RUSSIAN ARMS CONTROL CHEATING AND THE ADMINISTRATION'S RESPONSES

JOINT HEARING

BEFORE THE

SUBCOMMITTEE ON TERRORISM, NONPROLIFERATION, AND TRADE

OF THE

COMMITTEE ON FOREIGN AFFAIRS

(Serial No. 113–238)

AND THE

SUBCOMMITTEE ON STRATEGIC FORCES

OF THE

COMMITTEE ON ARMED SERVICES

(Serial No. 113–132)

HOUSE OF REPRESENTATIVES

ONE HUNDRED THIRTEENTH CONGRESS

SECOND SESSION

DECEMBER 10, 2014

Printed for the use of the Committee on Foreign Affairs and the Committee on Armed Services

Available via the World Wide Web: http://www.foreignaffairs.house.gov/ or http://www.gpo.gov/fdsys/

U.S. GOVERNMENT PUBLISHING OFFICE

91–846PDF   WASHINGTON : 2015

For sale by the Superintendent of Documents, U.S. Government Publishing Office
Internet: bookstore.gpo.gov   Phone: toll free (866) 512–1800; DC area (202) 512–1800
Fax: (202) 512–2104   Mail: Stop IDCC, Washington, DC 20402–0001

COMMITTEE ON FOREIGN AFFAIRS

EDWARD R. ROYCE, California, *Chairman*

CHRISTOPHER H. SMITH, New Jersey
ILEANA ROS-LEHTINEN, Florida
DANA ROHRABACHER, California
STEVE CHABOT, Ohio
JOE WILSON, South Carolina
MICHAEL T. McCAUL, Texas
TED POE, Texas
MATT SALMON, Arizona
TOM MARINO, Pennsylvania
JEFF DUNCAN, South Carolina
ADAM KINZINGER, Illinois
MO BROOKS, Alabama
TOM COTTON, Arkansas
PAUL COOK, California
GEORGE HOLDING, North Carolina
RANDY K. WEBER SR., Texas
SCOTT PERRY, Pennsylvania
STEVE STOCKMAN, Texas
RON DeSANTIS, Florida
DOUG COLLINS, Georgia
MARK MEADOWS, North Carolina
TED S. YOHO, Florida
SEAN DUFFY, Wisconsin
CURT CLAWSON, Florida

ELIOT L. ENGEL, New York
ENI F.H. FALEOMAVAEGA, American
  Samoa
BRAD SHERMAN, California
GREGORY W. MEEKS, New York
ALBIO SIRES, New Jersey
GERALD E. CONNOLLY, Virginia
THEODORE E. DEUTCH, Florida
BRIAN HIGGINS, New York
KAREN BASS, California
WILLIAM KEATING, Massachusetts
DAVID CICILLINE, Rhode Island
ALAN GRAYSON, Florida
JUAN VARGAS, California
BRADLEY S. SCHNEIDER, Illinois
JOSEPH P. KENNEDY III, Massachusetts
AMI BERA, California
ALAN S. LOWENTHAL, California
GRACE MENG, New York
LOIS FRANKEL, Florida
TULSI GABBARD, Hawaii
JOAQUIN CASTRO, Texas

AMY PORTER, *Chief of Staff*   THOMAS SHEEHY, *Staff Director*
JASON STEINBAUM, *Democratic Staff Director*

(II)

COMMITTEE ON FOREIGN AFFAIRS

SUBCOMMITTEE ON TERRORISM, NONPROLIFERATION, AND TRADE

TED POE, Texas, *Chairman*

JOE WILSON, South Carolina
ADAM KINZINGER, Illinois
MO BROOKS, Alabama
TOM COTTON, Arkansas
PAUL COOK, California
SCOTT PERRY, Pennsylvania
TED S. YOHO, Florida

BRAD SHERMAN, California
ALAN S. LOWENTHAL, California
JOAQUIN CASTRO, Texas
JUAN VARGAS, California
BRADLEY S. SCHNEIDER, Illinois
JOSEPH P. KENNEDY III, Massachusetts

————

COMMITTEE ON ARMED SERVICES

SUBCOMMITTEE ON STRATEGIC FORCES

MIKE ROGERS, Alabama, *Chairman*

TRENT FRANKS, Arizona
DOUG LAMBORN, Colorado
MIKE COFFMAN, Colorado
MO BROOKS, Alabama
JOE WILSON, South Carolina
MICHAEL R. TURNER, Ohio
JOHN FLEMING, Louisiana
RICHARD B. NUGENT, Florida
JIM BRIDENSTINE, Oklahoma

JIM COOPER, Tennessee
LORETTA SANCHEZ, California
JAMES R. LANGEVIN, Rhode Island
RICK LARSEN, Washington
JOHN GARAMENDI, California
HENRY C. "HANK" JOHNSON, JR., Georgia
ANDRÉ CARSON, Indiana
MARC A. VEASEY, Texas

TIM MORRISON, *Counsel*
LEONOR TOMERO, *Counsel*
COLIN BOSSE AND ERIC SMITH, *Clerks*

CONTENTS

RUSSIAN ARMS CONTROL CHEATING AND THE ADMINISTRATION'S RESPONSES

WEDNESDAY, DECEMBER 10, 2014

House of Representatives,
Subcommittee on Terrorism, Nonproliferation, and Trade,
Committee on Foreign Affairs and
Subcommittee on Strategic Forces,
Committee on Armed Services,

Washington, DC.

The subcommittees met, pursuant to notice, at 2:01 p.m., in room 2118, Rayburn House Office Building, Hon. Ted Poe (chairman of the subcommittee) presiding.

Mr. POE. The Subcommittee on Terrorism, Nonproliferation, and Trade and the Subcommittee on Strategic Forces is convened.

This hearing is a continuation of the Russians' arms control to bring us up to date. I would recall and remind all committee members that there was a classified briefing yesterday on this issue. We have this public briefing today, and there will be another classified briefing after this public hearing this afternoon. The classified briefing I found alarming, and that is why we have the witnesses here this morning, or this afternoon.

The Chair, with the agreement of Mr. Rogers, will dispense with all opening statements of members. Without objection, all of the members may have 5 days to submit statements, questions, and extraneous materials for the record subject to the length of limitation in the rules.

I will introduce our two witnesses, allow them to give their statements. Then we will recess for votes and come back for questions. That will be the format of this joint committee hearing.

Ms. Rose Gottemoeller is the Under Secretary for Arms Control and International Security at the U.S. Department of State. Mrs. Gottemoeller also served as the Assistant Secretary of State for the Bureau of Arms Control, Verification and Compliance, and was the chief U.S. negotiator in the New START treaty with Russia.

Mr. Brian McKeon is the Principal Deputy Under Secretary for Policy at the U.S. Department of Defense. Mr. McKeon also served on the National Security Council staff and as Deputy National Security Advisor to the Vice President.

Ms. Gottemoeller, we will start with you.

I would request that the witnesses try to keep their statements to 5 minutes.

You are recognized.

STATEMENT OF THE HONORABLE ROSE GOTTEMOELLER, UNDER SECRETARY FOR ARMS CONTROL AND INTERNATIONAL SECURITY, U.S. DEPARTMENT OF STATE

Ms. GOTTEMOELLER. Thank you very much, Mr. Chairman.

Chairmen Poe and Rogers, Ranking Members Sherman and Cooper, distinguished members of the House Foreign Affairs and Armed Services Committees, thank you for hosting this hearing today, for having me here today.

Today I want to seek about three things: Why arms control agreements with Russia continue to be an important tool to enhance the security of the United States, our allies, and partners; the seriousness with which the administration takes compliance with arms control agreements; and U.S. efforts to ensure Russian compliance with its arms control obligations.

As has been recognized for 4 decades, verifiable arms control agreements can enhance the security of the United States, our allies, and our partners. The Obama administration has continued the longstanding bipartisan approach to arms control with Russia that had its origins in the days of the cold war. The administrations of President Ronald Reagan and George H.W. Bush were the architects of many of our most successful and enduring arms control efforts.

That said, Russia's actions in Ukraine, increasingly confrontational posture, and violations of the INF and CFE treaties have undermined trust and must be addressed. While diplomacy between the United States and Russia continues, no one can ignore that Russia's actions have undermined the very principles upon which cooperation is built.

Further, as we consider arms control priorities this year or in any year, we will continue to consult closely with our allies and partners at every step of the way. Our security and defense, as well as that of our allies and partners, is nonnegotiable. We will only support arms control agreements that advance our national security interests.

I will cite the New START example as one such. Since New START entered into force in 2011, the United States has inspected, with boots on the ground, Russian nuclear weapons facilities 70 times. Moreover, the United States and Russian Federation have exchanged more than 7,500 notifications on one another's nuclear forces in the past 4 years. These notifications provide predictability by enabling the tracking of strategic offensive arms from location to location, giving advance notice of upcoming of ballistic missile test launches, and providing updates of changes in the status of systems covered by the treaty.

In the realm of conventional arms control, the United States and our allies have been using arms control and confidence-building mechanisms in an effort to promote stability in Europe, provide transparency on Russia's provocative actions in and around Ukraine, and assure our allies and partners in the face of Russian aggression.

We believe that arms control mechanisms have great importance not only in providing insight and transparency into Russian actions on the ground in and around Ukraine but in demonstrating support for our allies and partners. More broadly, such mechanisms contribute to greater transparency and stability in the Euro-Atlantic region.

I want to underscore, Mr. Chairman and colleagues, that our NATO allies and other partners in Europe are strong supporters of arms control and confidence-building mechanisms. And they count on our active participation and leadership of these efforts.

Now let me turn very quickly to INF.

In July of this year, as you know, the United States announced its determination that Russia was in violation of its Intermediate-Range Nuclear Forces Treaty obligations not to posses, produce, or flight-test a ground-launched cruise missile with a range capability of 500 to 5,500 kilometers. We take this violation extremely seriously.

The INF Treaty, negotiated and ratified during the Reagan administration, eliminated an entire class of ballistic and cruise missiles capable of delivering nuclear and nonnuclear weapons. The INF Treaty benefits the security of the United States, our allies, and the Russian Federation, and the United States is committed to the continued viability of the INF Treaty.

We have been steadily raising our concerns with Russia regarding violation of the INF Treaty and have, since July, held senior-level bilateral discussions, with the aim of returning Russia to verifiable compliance with its treaty obligations.

In addition to these diplomatic efforts, we are actively reviewing potential economic measures in response to Russia's violation, and the United States is assessing options in the military sphere to ensure that Russia will not gain a significant military advantage from its violation of the INF Treaty.

My colleague, Brian McKeon, will speak further about that.

In sum, for more than 40 years, arms control has been a tool that has contributed substantially to the national security interests of the United States, providing predictability and stability to us and to the global community. As owners of more than 90 percent of the nuclear global stockpile, the United States and Russia continue to have a special responsibility in this regard.

We will continue to pursue arms control and nonproliferation tools along with effective verification, because they are the best path that we can take to effectively limit and reduce nuclear threats and prevent such weapons from proliferating to other nation-states or falling into the hands of extremists bent on causing colossal destruction.

Thank you for your partnership in this effort, and I look forward to answering your questions.

Thank you, Mr. Chairman.

[The prepared statement of Ms. Gottemoeller follows:]

Rose E. Gottemoeller
Under Secretary of Arms Control and International Security

Testimony

Joint Hearing
House Foreign Affairs Committee, Subcommittee on Terrorism,
Nonproliferation, and Trade
House Armed Services Committee, Subcommittee on Strategic Forces

Rayburn House Office Building
December 10, 2014

Chairmen Poe and Rogers, Ranking Members Sherman and Cooper, distinguished Members of the House Foreign Affairs and Armed Services Committees. Thank you for hosting this hearing and for having me here today.

Today, I want to speak to you about:

1) why arms control agreements with Russia continue to be an important tool to enhance the security of the United States, our allies, and partners;

2) the seriousness with which the Administration takes compliance with arms control agreements; and

3) U.S. efforts to ensure Russian compliance with its arms control obligations.

As has been recognized for over four decades, verifiable arms control agreements can enhance the security of the United States, our Allies, and our partners. It is one of the many diplomatic, military and economic tools that the United States uses to address 21st Century challenges. We have worked closely with our Allies and partners to develop the arms control framework we have today. The United States and its allies are made safer and more secure by such agreements as they limit weapons and their destructive potential for all parties to the agreement, while providing transparency and predictability. The Obama Administration has continued the longstanding bipartisan approach to arms control with Russia that had its origins in the days of the Cold War. The administrations of Presidents Ronald Reagan and George H.W. Bush were the architects of many of our most successful and enduring arms control efforts.

Our overall approach to strategic stability with Russia remains unchanged since the Cold War: the United States is committed to maintaining strategic stability between the United States and Russia. This is because it is, without a doubt, in the national security interest of the United States and our allies to do so.

That said, Russia's aggressive actions in Ukraine, increasingly confrontational posture, and violations of the INF and CFE Treaties have undermined trust and must be addressed. While diplomacy between the United States and Russia continues, no one can ignore that Russia's actions have undermined the very principles upon which cooperation is built. Further, as we consider arms control priorities this year or in any year, we will continue to consult closely with our allies and partners every step of the way. Our security and defense, as well as that of our allies and partners, is non-negotiable. We will only support arms control agreements that advance our national security interests.

During the Cold War, Washington and Moscow found it in our mutual interest to work together to limit or ban certain systems, and to cap and then to begin to reduce the number of nuclear weapons to reverse the nuclear arms race and improve mutual security and stability. For the same reasons, we judged that the New START Treaty was in the U.S. national security interest, and we continue to judge that the New START Treaty remains in the U.S. national security interest today. We are now in the fourth year of implementation and, despite the crisis in Ukraine, we and Russia continue to implement the Treaty in a business-like manner. Furthermore, as outlined in our 2014 New START Treaty Implementation Report, the Russian Federation is in compliance with its obligations under the New START Treaty.

Since New START entered into force in 2011, the United States has inspected—with boots on the ground—Russian nuclear weapons facilities 70 times. Moreover, the United States and the Russian Federation have exchanged more than 7500 notifications on one another's nuclear forces in the last four years. These notifications provide predictability by enabling the tracking of strategic offensive arms from location to location, giving advance notice of upcoming ballistic missile test launches, and providing updates of changes in the status of systems covered by the Treaty. For example, a notification is sent every time a heavy bomber is moved out of its home base for more than 24 hours. Additionally, when either party conducts a flight test of an ICBM or SLBM, they are required to notify the other party one day in advance.

The Treaty's verification mechanisms allow us to monitor and inspect Russia's strategic nuclear forces to ensure compliance with the Treaty. For both the United States and Russia, accurate and timely knowledge of each other's nuclear forces helps to prevent the risks of misunderstandings, mistrust, worst-case analysis, and worst-case policymaking. Put another way, the New START Treaty's verification regime is a vital tool in ensuring transparency and predictability between the world's largest nuclear powers. During times of heightened tensions overall, such predictability and transparency only becomes more important.

In the realm of conventional arms control, the United States and our Allies have been using arms control and confidence building mechanisms in an effort to promote stability in Europe, provide transparency on Russia's provocative actions in and around Ukraine, and assure our allies and partners in the face of Russian aggression. For example, the Vienna Document on Confidence and Security Building Measures has been used by our Allies and partners – and by the United States – to gain insight into Russia's military actions. Vienna Document inspections provided a near-continuous presence in Ukraine from March through June of this year, providing reassurance to Ukraine and insight into the situation on the ground, particularly in the weeks before the OSCE's Special Monitoring Mission was in place.

Additionally, the United States has worked with NATO Allies and other Open Skies Treaty partners to conduct observation flights over western Russia and additional flights over Ukraine in order to provide reassurance to Ukraine and gain insight into reported Russian military activity.

We believe these arms control mechanisms have great importance not only in providing insight and transparency into Russian actions in and around Ukraine, but demonstrating support for our allies and partners. More broadly, such mechanisms contribute to greater transparency and stability in the Euro-Atlantic region.

I want to underscore that our NATO allies and other partners in Europe are strong supporters of arms control and confidence building mechanisms in Europe and they count on our active participation and leadership in those efforts.

And furthermore, when Russia – or any other nation – does not uphold its arms control obligations, we hold them accountable. For example, Russia ceased implementation of its Conventional Armed Forces in Europe Treaty (CFE) obligations in December 2007. After two intensive diplomatic efforts to break the impasse and encourage Russia to resume implementation, in November 2011, the

United States responded to Russia's violation of its obligations by suspending U.S. performance of certain obligations under the CFE Treaty as to Russia. We were joined by our NATO Allies that are party to the Treaty, as well as Georgia and Moldova, in taking this step – in all, 24 of the 30 countries that are party to the Treaty have suspended implementation of certain CFE obligations with Russia.

So, let me assure this committee that the Administration takes compliance with all arms control agreements extremely seriously. For this reason, this Administration worked hard to produce a compliance report in July of 2010 – the first delivered to Congress after a five year lapse – and has produced one every year since. Prior to this Administration, 2005 was the last year that a report had been delivered to Congress.

While the State Department has the lead in drafting the report, the Department of Defense contributes and is fully consulted throughout the process, as mandated by the Arms Control and Disarmament Act. Producing the compliance report also requires input from the Intelligence Community and the Department of Energy.

As part of this process, In July of this year, the United States announced its determination that Russia is in violation of its INF Treaty obligations not to possess, produce, or flight-test a ground-launched cruise missile with a range capability of 500 to 5,500 kilometers, or to possess or produce launchers of such missiles.

We take this violation extremely seriously. The INF Treaty, negotiated and ratified during the Reagan Administration, eliminated an entire class of ballistic and cruise missiles, capable of delivering nuclear and non-nuclear weapons. The INF Treaty benefits the security of the United States, our allies, and the Russian Federation. The United States is committed to making every effort to ensure the continued viability of the INF Treaty.

We have raised with Russia our concerns regarding its violation of the INF Treaty and have since held senior-level bilateral discussions with the aim of returning Russia to verifiable compliance with its Treaty obligations.

To date, Russia has been unwilling to acknowledge its violation or address our concerns. Therefore, we are reviewing a series of diplomatic, economic, and military measures to protect the interests of the United States and our Allies, and encourage Russia to uphold its nuclear arms control commitments. First, the United States is engaging diplomatically with Russia as noted above, and we continue to consult closely with our Allies. Let me underscore that our Allies have made clear their interest in preserving the INF Treaty. On September 5, at the NATO Summit in Wales, Allies noted:

"it is of paramount importance that disarmament and non-proliferation commitments under existing treaties are honoured, including the Intermediate-Range Nuclear Forces (INF) Treaty, which is a crucial element of Euro-Atlantic security. In that regard, Allies call on Russia to preserve the viability of the INF Treaty through ensuring full and verifiable compliance."

Second, we are actively reviewing potential economic measures in response to Russia's violation. And third, the United States is assessing options in the military sphere to ensure that Russia would not gain a significant military advantage from its violation of the INF Treaty.

Currently, there is debate in Russia about its nuclear modernization programs and about the contribution of the INF Treaty to Russia's security. It is important for Russia to take into account that no military decisions happen in a vacuum. Actions beget actions. Our countries have been down the road of needless, costly, and destabilizing arms races. We know where that road leads, and we are fortunate that our past leaders had the wisdom and strength to turn us in a new direction. We will keep pressing the Russian leadership to come back into compliance with all of its international obligations.

I would like to assure this committee that the Obama Administration is committed to bringing Russia back into compliance with the INF Treaty. We will not waver in this effort. But the security of the United States and its allies is not negotiable. We must also take steps to ensure our continued collective security should Russia continue in this violation of its INF obligations.

But just as during the Cold War, we will not allow Russia's bad actions in one arena to compromise U.S. national security in another. For more than 40 years, arms control has been a tool that has contributed substantially to the national security interest of the United States, providing predictability and stability to us and to the global community. As the owners of more than 90% of the global nuclear stockpile, the United States and Russia continue to have a special responsibility to protect and preserve those regimes. We will continue to pursue arms control and nonproliferation tools – along with effective verification mechanisms – because they are the best path that we can take to effectively limit and reduce nuclear threats and prevent such weapons from proliferating to other nation states or falling into the hands of extremists bent on causing colossal destruction. We are committed to monitoring and ensuring compliance with these agreements, and we will continue to tirelessly press Russia to return to its obligations under the INF Treaty. At the same time, we will continue to assess all of the tools—military, economic, and diplomatic—available to the United States and its allies to ensure our national security. And of course we will continue to consult with Congress and our allies and partners on these efforts.

Thank you for your partnership in this effort, and I look forward to answering your questions.

———————

Mr. POE. The Chair recognizes Mr. McKeon for 5 minutes.

STATEMENT OF THE HONORABLE BRIAN MCKEON, PRINCIPAL DEPUTY UNDER SECRETARY FOR POLICY, U.S. DEPARTMENT OF DEFENSE

Mr. MCKEON. Thank you very much, sir.

Chairman Rogers, Chairman Poe, Ranking Member Cooper, Ranking Member Sherman, distinguished members of the two subcommittees, thank you for this opportunity today.

I will try not to repeat what Under Secretary Gottemoeller has told you. In addressing the issues outlined in your letter of invitation, I would point you to my full statement for the record. Let me highlight a few key points.

When implemented fully by all parties, arms control agreements advance U.S. national security interests. The United States is made safer and more secure by such agreements. The administration closely monitors compliance of other states-parties to arms control treaties and agreements, including that of the Russian Federation. And, as required by law, we report this assessment to the Congress.

Through this effort, the Obama administration has determined that the Russian Federation is in violation of its obligations under the INF Treaty. We reported this violation in the arms control compliance report issued in 2014, and we have briefed you regularly on our concerns about Russia's actions and discussed it with our allies and partners.

We believe the INF Treaty contributes not only to U.S. and Russian security but also to that of our allies and partners. For that reason, Russian possession, development, or deployment of a weapons system in violation of the treaty will not be ignored.

Our objective from the very beginning has been to preserve the viability of the INF Treaty and convince Russia to come back into compliance with its obligations under it. Our approach to this issue has been multipronged, beginning with engaging Russia diplomatically while discussing other potential measures in coordination with allies.

We have engaged the Russian Federation in diplomatic channels since 2013, including senior-level discussions in Moscow in September of this year. Unfortunately, Russia has not been forthcoming with any information, nor has it acknowledged the existence of a noncompliant cruise missile. Instead, the Russian side has chosen to accuse the United States of violating its obligations under the INF Treaty.

In our view, all of Russia's claims are categorically unfounded. The United States has been and remains in compliance with all of its obligations under the INF Treaty. In our September meeting in Moscow, we fully addressed each of Russia's concerns, providing Russian officials with detailed explanations and treaty-based reasons as to how U.S. actions comply with our obligations. These Russian claims, we believe, are meant to divert attention from its own violation.

As a result of Russia's actions, the Joint Staff has conducted a military assessment of the threat were Russia to deploy an INF Treaty-range ground-launched cruise missile in Europe or the Asia-

Pacific region. This assessment has led us to review a broad range of military response options and consider the effect each option could have on convincing Russian leadership to return to compliance with the INF Treaty as well as countering the capability of a Russian INF Treaty-prohibited system.

We do not want to find ourselves engaged in an escalatory cycle of action and reaction. However, Russia's lack of meaningful engagement on this issue, if it persists, will ultimately require the United States to take actions to protect its interests and security, along with those of its allies and partners. Those actions will make Russia less secure.

We now have a significant challenge ahead of us. We hope the Russia Federation will remember why the Soviet Union signed the INF Treaty in the first place. By agreeing to that treaty, the United States and the Soviet Union ensured that both parties benefited from the removal of weapons systems that posed a real and credible threat to European security.

As I noted at the outset, the United States takes treaty compliance very seriously. The ramifications of Russia's actions and our response affect more than just one arms control agreement; they affect our ability to pursue future arms control and nonproliferation regimes. Such a violation threatens our security and the collective security of many allies and partners. This violation will not go unanswered, because there is too much at stake.

We look forward to keeping you informed on this matter as the situation develops.

Thank you for the opportunity to be here today, and we look forward to your questions.

[The prepared statement of Mr. McKeon follows:]

STATEMENT OF

HONORABLE BRIAN P. MCKEON
PRINCIPAL DEPUTY UNDER SECRETARY OF DEFENSE
FOR POLICY

BEFORE THE HOUSE
COMMITTEE ON ARMED SERVICES
SUBCOMMITTEE ON STRATEGIC FORCES
AND
COMMITTEE ON FOREIGN AFFAIRS
SUBCOMMITTEE ON TERRORISM, NONPROLIFERATION, AND TRADE

DECEMBER 10, 2014

Chairman Rogers, Chairman Poe, Ranking Member Cooper, Ranking Member Sherman, distinguished members of the Strategic Forces Subcommittee and Terrorism, Nonproliferation, and Trade Subcommittee, thank you for the opportunity to testify on Russian arms control compliance.

You asked me to describe current compliance by the Russian Federation with its arms control agreements and obligations and, in the cases of noncompliance, how the Administration is responding to and holding the Russian Federation accountable for its actions. In particular, you have asked me to describe Russia's noncompliance with the Intermediate-Range Nuclear Forces (INF) Treaty and the Administration's response to this violation, including coordinating with our allies and partners in Europe and in the Asia-Pacific region.

Arms control improves U.S. national security by stabilizing the strategic balance between the United States and other nations at lower levels of weapons. The United States is made safer and more secure by such agreements.

Adherence by all parties to their treaty commitments is central to the effectiveness of such agreements. Issues of noncompliance must be addressed – and resolved – with our treaty partners. This involves a full interagency process in evaluating occurrences of noncompliance and aggressively responding to them in order to preserve the credibility and viability of the treaty regime.

The 2014 Compliance Report

The Report on Adherence to and Compliance with Arms Control, Nonproliferation, and Disarmament Agreements and Commitments is a critical part of this process. The report covering calendar year 2013 was released by the Department of State in July 2014 and will be referred to as the 2014 Compliance Report.

In addition to including a detailed assessment of adherence of the United States to obligations in arms control, nonproliferation, and disarmament agreements, the statutorily required Compliance Report comprehensively assesses the compliance of other nations with their obligations under such agreements. Although this report was prepared for the President by the Secretary of State, the Secretary of Defense was fully consulted on the preparation of the report as required by the Arms Control and Disarmament Act. The Office of the Secretary of Defense continues to take a very active role, along with the full interagency, in assisting the Department of State in the preparation of this very important report.

The Department of Defense (DoD) is responsible for overseeing DoD compliance with all U.S. arms control, nonproliferation, and disarmament agreements and commitments. DoD components ensure their various program offices adhere to department compliance directives. We have a robust compliance review process that ensures programs and activities comply with U.S. international obligations. Interagency consultation on DoD programs is also conducted in appropriate cases.

As a result of this diligence, the United States is in compliance with all its obligations under arms control, nonproliferation, and disarmament agreements and commitments, and continues to make every effort to comply with them.

Russian Compliance

The administration closely monitors the compliance of other States Parties, including that of the Russian Federation, to treaties and agreements. The 2014 Compliance Report chronicles concerns about Russian noncompliance with its obligations under a number of treaties and agreements. These include the Biological and Toxin Weapons Convention, the Threshold Test Ban Treaty, the Treaty on Conventional Armed Forces in Europe, the Treaty on Open Skies, and the INF Treaty. While assessed in a separate report, the Chemical Weapons Convention also falls in this category

My comments today will focus on Russia's violation of its INF Treaty obligations, but first I would like to address the New START Treaty.

New START Treaty

We assess that the Russian Federation is in compliance with its obligations under the New START Treaty. Despite the recent downturn in the U.S.–Russian relationship, implementation of the New START Treaty has proceeded with no recognizable change in its implementation. The United States and Russia continue to conduct their full quota of inspections and exchange information on numbers and status of their strategic forces. Both sides also continue to meet under the Treaty's Bilateral Consultative Commission to address issues related to implementation of the Treaty.

The New START Treaty enhances U.S. national security by providing predictability and stability in the strategic balance between the United States and the Russian Federation at lower levels of strategic nuclear forces. The Treaty's verification regime continues to provide visibility into and insights on Russia's strategic forces.

For our part, the United States remains in full compliance with its obligations under the New START Treaty. As such, we continue to work toward implementing the objectives of the

2010 Nuclear Posture Review and achieving the final New START Treaty force structure by the Treaty's February 2018 deadline. I particularly thank the Subcommittee on Strategic Forces for your continued support of the nuclear forces and the nuclear enterprise.

Intermediate-Range Nuclear Forces Treaty

For my remaining time, I want to describe our serious concerns regarding the Russian Federation's noncompliance with its obligations under the INF Treaty and the actions we are taking to resolve this important issue.

The INF Treaty entered into force in 1988 and is a treaty originally between the United States and the Soviet Union. It exists now as a treaty between the United States and twelve successor States to the former Soviet Union, one of them being the Russian Federation. The INF Treaty required the Parties to eliminate and permanently forswear nuclear and conventionally-armed ground-launched ballistic missiles (GLBM) and cruise missiles (GLCM) with ranges from 500 km to 5,500 kilometers, along with their launchers, and associated support structures and equipment. The INF Treaty specifically prohibits the possession, production, and flight-testing of such missiles. It also prohibits the possession or production of any launchers for such missiles. The INF Treaty places no restrictions on manned aircraft, air-launched or sea-launched systems, or ground-launched systems with ranges less than 500 km or greater than 5,500 km. It is important to note ground-launched ballistic missiles with ranges greater than 5,500 km and submarine-launched ballistic missiles with ranges greater than 600 km are limited under New START.

Russia's Violation of the INF Treaty

The Administration has determined that the Russian Federation is in violation of its obligations under the INF Treaty not to possess, produce, or flight-test a GLCM with a range capability of 500 km to 5,500 km, or to possess or produce launchers of such missiles.

We have briefed you regularly on our concerns about Russia's actions and discussed it with our allies and partners.

We have engaged the Russian Federation in diplomatic discussions since early 2013, including senior-level discussions in Moscow in September 2014. We have conveyed to Russian officials we expect the Russian Federation to cease any further development, testing, production, and deployment of this noncompliant system and to eliminate the missiles and launchers in a verifiable manner. Unfortunately, Russia has not been forthcoming with any information, nor has it acknowledged the existence of such a noncompliant cruise missile.

We believe it is in the mutual security interests of the United States and all the Parties to the INF Treaty that they all remain Parties to the Treaty and uphold their obligations. The INF Treaty contributes not only to the parties' security, but also to that of U.S. allies and partners, and to regional security and stability in Europe and in the Asia-Pacific region. Russian possession, development, or deployment of a weapons system in violation of the INF Treaty will not be ignored.

U.S. Response to Russia's INF Treaty Violation

From the moment we determined that we had a concern with a new Russian program, our objective has been to preserve the viability of the INF Treaty and convince Russia to come back into compliance with its obligations. This means Russia must cease its noncompliant activity and eliminate all INF Treaty-prohibited missiles and launchers in a verifiable manner.

Our approach to this issue has been multipronged, beginning with engaging Russia diplomatically while discussing potential economic measures in coordination with allies. Consideration of other response options has always been part of our strategy as well and I can address that aspect in more detail during the closed session.

Diplomatic Engagement with the Russian Federation:

We began raising our concerns with Russia in May 2013 and have repeated them on numerous occasions since that time. Most of these interactions have been carried out by my State Department colleagues.

Since the release of the 2014 Compliance Report in July of this year, the United States has engaged at senior levels with the Russian Federation in an attempt to move constructively toward resolving our concerns and convincing Russia to return to compliance. Shortly after the release of the Report, Secretary Hagel discussed the violation with his counterpart, Russian Minister of Defense Shoygu. Chairman Dempsey had a similar conversation with General Gerasimov, Chief of the Russian General Staff. Following these interactions, Russian President Putin accepted President Obama's suggestion of having senior-level teams convene to discuss this matter.

In September of this year, Under Secretary Gottemoeller led a senior U.S. delegation to Moscow to discuss the concerns of both sides regarding compliance with the INF Treaty. I attended for the Office of the Secretary of Defense along with a full interagency team. We had a frank exchange, but the meetings did not resolve our concerns. We will continue to pursue a dialogue with the Russian Federation on this serious matter.

Military Assessment and Military Response Options

As a result of Russia's actions, the Joint Staff has conducted a military assessment of the threat if Russia were to deploy an INF Treaty-range ground-launched cruise missile in Europe or the Asia-Pacific region. This assessment will continue to be updated as developments warrant.

The assessment tells us that development and deployment of such a system by the Russian Federation would pose a threat to the United States and its allies and partners.

The Joint Staff assessment has led us to review a broad range of military response options and consider the effect each option could have on convincing Russian leadership to return to compliance with the INF Treaty, as well as countering the capability of a Russian INF Treaty-prohibited system.

I can go into more detail on the military assessment in the closed session.

Russian Allegations of U.S. Noncompliance with the INF Treaty

Shortly after we began raising our concerns with Russia regarding violation of its INF Treaty obligations, the Russian side began formally accusing the United States of violating its obligations under the INF Treaty. Russia raised some of these allegations in the past, but has not done so formally for many years. All of Russia's claims, past and present, are categorically unfounded. The United States has been and remains in compliance with all of its obligations under the INF Treaty. These Russian claims are meant to divert attention from its own violation.

We fully addressed each of Russia's concerns during the September 11 meetings in Moscow, and provided the Russian side with detailed explanations and Treaty-based explanations as to how U.S. actions are compliant with our obligations under the Treaty.

Specifically, the Russians have accused the United States of violating its obligations as a result of three different activities.

First, the Russian side claims that certain U.S. ballistic target missiles are not compliant with INF Treaty provisions.

The United States uses various booster configurations to simulate certain aspects of threat missiles for the purpose of testing our missile defense systems. The purpose of these tests is research and development of missile defense systems, not the development of the target boosters systems into banned offensive missiles. The INF Treaty explicitly permits the use of older booster stages for research and development purposes subject to specific Treaty rules. This includes their use as targets for missile defense tests.

Second, the Russian Federation, despite its own development of such systems, claims that armed, unmanned aerial vehicles, or UAVs, are ground-launched cruise missiles and therefore banned by the INF Treaty.

The United States employs a number of armed versions of UAVs. All of them are two-way, reusable systems. The INF Treaty imposes no restrictions on the testing, production, or possession of two-way, reusable, armed UAVs. Such UAVs are not missiles and, therefore, are not covered by the INF Treaty.

Third, Russia claims that the launcher complex for the Aegis Ashore missile defense system is capable of launching Tomahawk cruise missiles. A launcher with such a capability would be prohibited under the INF Treaty.

The Aegis Ashore missile defense system is fully consistent, and complies with U.S. obligations under the INF Treaty. The Aegis Ashore vertical launching system is not the same launcher as the sea-based Mk-41 Vertical Launching System, although it utilizes some of the same structural components as the sea-based system. Equally important, the Aegis Ashore system is only capable of launching defensive interceptor missiles, such as the SM-3. It is incapable of launching cruise missiles.

Despite our explanations, the Russian Federation says that it remains unconvinced and continues to assert its claims about our activities.

Reassuring Allies and Partners

We have also kept our allies informed of Russia's violation and its implications. After our meeting in Moscow in September, Under Secretary Gottemoeller briefed the North Atlantic Council by a secure videoconference call. We continue to consult our European and Asian allies and partners as we assess the political and military implications of Russia's actions and discuss the need for and the type of possible responses. Reassuring our allies and partners of our commitment to our collective security is essential as we develop our responses to Russia's violations, and we will continue to stress the importance of building a strong, international consensus in responding to it.

Review of Policy toward Russia

It is also important we consider Russian actions with regard to the INF Treaty in the context of its overall behavior.

Ongoing assessments within the Administration are not only looking at Russia's INF Treaty violation, but are seeking to develop a comprehensive Russia policy in light of other Russian actions, including those in Ukraine. We are insisting Russia abide by its international agreements, and the Administration continues to evaluate its overall strategy toward Russia taking into account all of Russia's activities. We will not ignore Russia's actions. The United States has made this clear to the Russian Federation.

We do not want to find ourselves engaged in an escalatory action/reaction cycle as a result of Russia's decision to possess INF Treaty-prohibited weapons. However, Russia's lack of meaningful engagement on this issue, if it persists, will ultimately require the United States to take actions to protect its interests and security along with those of its allies and partners. Those actions will make Russia less secure.

Conclusion

In conclusion, we have a significant challenge ahead of us. Since 2009, we have engaged Russia on taking mutually beneficial steps for enhancing strategic stability. Similarly, with our allies and partners we have made considerable progress in strengthening extended deterrence and assurance.

We believe this pursuit of strategic stability remains in the interest of both the United States and Russia, and we hope the Russian Federation will remember why the Soviet Union signed onto the INF Treaty in the first place. By agreeing to the Treaty, the United States and the Soviet Union ensured that both Parties benefited from the removal of weapon systems that posed a real and credible threat to European security. The reintroduction of such weapons systems is destabilizing, and not in the interests of the United States, Europe, Asia, or the Russian Federation.

The United States takes treaty compliance very seriously. The ramifications of Russia's actions and our response affect more than just one arms control agreement. They affect our ability to pursue future arms control and nonproliferation regimes. Such a violation threatens the national security and collective security of many allies and partners, and, ultimately, Russia's actions affect strategic stability. This violation will not go unanswered because there is too much at stake.

We look forward to keeping you informed on this matter as the situation develops. Thank you for the opportunity to testify. I look forward to your questions.

———

Mr. POE. I thank the statements of the witnesses.

As previously stated, the subcommittees will be in recess until 15 minutes after the last vote in a series of three votes. The first series—or the first vote in the series is taking place now.

So the subcommittees are adjourned.

[Recess.]

Mr. POE. The subcommittees will come to order.

The Chair will recognize himself for 5 minutes.

If I understand your testimony correctly, the Russians are in violation of this treaty. My question is, are the Russians in violation of any other arms control treaties besides the INF?

Ms. GOTTEMOELLER. Yes, Mr. Chairman. We do consider the Russians to be in violation of the Conventional Forces in Europe Treaty.

Mr. POE. Is it correct to say that the Russians are in violation, are not complying with the eight other arms control treaties besides this one?

Ms. GOTTEMOELLER. Sir, in some cases, we are working on compliance issues with them. In the case of the Open Skies Treaty, for example, we have had some concerns about their compliance with the Open Skies Treaty, but we are working, and in some cases successfully working, to resolve some of our concerns.

In other cases, such as the Biological Weapons Convention, we have been unable to determine whether current activities that they have going on would not be in compliance with the treaty. And in some cases——

Mr. POE. Excuse me. Let me ask you this question.

Ms. GOTTEMOELLER. Yes.

Mr. POE. Are they in violation or not in compliance with eight other arms control treaties?

Ms. GOTTEMOELLER. Sir, I believe that is not quite correct, because some we have determined that they are in violation, actually in violation of the treaty, and in some cases there are some issues that we are working with them on to determine their compliance.

Mr. POE. Does not being in compliance mean the same as violation?

Ms. GOTTEMOELLER. Well, I will just give you an example, sir. We have for each of the treaties and agreements an implementation body for that treaty or agreement. In the case of the New START treaty, it is called the Bilateral Consultative Commission. And when issues come up in an inspection, we may have a difference with the Russians, but we try to sit down and work out that difference. In the latest session of the BCC, we were able to work out some differences with the Russians about their inspection approaches.

So it takes some time and it takes some work to figure out whether they are actually in violation of a treaty.

Mr. POE. So does "violation" and "noncompliance" mean different things? That is really my question.

Ms. GOTTEMOELLER. "Violation" and "noncompliance" mean the same thing. I was just making the point that, in each of the treaties and agreements, if we went through them one by one, I could tell you, you know, in some cases——

Mr. POE. So——

Ms. GOTTEMOELLER [continuing]. We are working——

Mr. POE [continuing]. Let's go back to my question.

Ms. GOTTEMOELLER [continuing]. On issues.

Mr. POE. I am sorry. I want to get this straight. "Noncompliance" and "violation" do mean the same thing.

Ms. GOTTEMOELLER. Correct, sir.

Mr. POE. So are the Russians in violation and are not in compliance with eight other treaties?

Ms. GOTTEMOELLER. Sir, they are not in compliance or in violation with the INF Treaty and the CFE Treaty. In certain other cases, we have concerns that we are working with them on.

Mr. POE. So is it "yes" or "no," as far as eight treaties?

Ms. GOTTEMOELLER. I do not believe the number is eight, sir. It is "no" for eight treaties.

Mr. POE. If the Russians are in violation of the INF Treaty—and you have testified that they are in violation—the United States has options. One of those options is to withdraw from the INF Treaty; is that correct?

Ms. GOTTEMOELLER. That is correct. And, in fact, the United States has a right to withdraw in any event. It is one of the articles of the treaty. We always put that in for national security purposes, a country may choose to withdraw from a treaty.

Mr. POE. And what is the United States position on—what is our position today on withdrawing from the INF Treaty? We know they are in violation. Are we going to withdraw from the treaty?

Ms. GOTTEMOELLER. Our view is that it is in the national security interests of the United States and of our allies and partners to remain in the INF Treaty and to work to bring Russia back into full compliance with the treaty.

Mr. POE. How long are we going to give the Russians to come back to the fold, so to speak? A month? A year? Ten years? When are we going to make the decision, you have had enough time to come into compliance after you are in clear violation, this is the day of reckoning? How long are we going to give them to come into compliance?

Ms. GOTTEMOELLER. Sir, I can't tell you exactly. We have a diplomatic effort going on.

I can give you two historical examples. In the case of the ABM Treaty, the Reagan administration and the Bush administration worked with the Soviets diplomatically for 5 years before they were able to bring the Russians back into compliance with that treaty.

In the case of the CFE Treaty, the Bush administration, George W. Bush administration, and the Obama administration also worked for 5 years. And, in that case, we did not bring the Russians back into compliance with the treaty. We declared countermeasures, and, basically, we have now put in place countermeasures against the Russians with regard to the—with regard to the CFE Treaty.

Mr. POE. Two more questions.

It is my understanding that we first detected Russian violations of the INF Treaty in 2008. If I do my math correctly, that is 6 years.

I am no expert in arms, but I would think the Russians would lather up with the idea that they are in violation, continue to be in violation, and we are just going to keep postponing a decision to withdraw from the treaty.

What other options do we have besides withdrawing from the treaty?

Ms. GOTTEMOELLER. Sir, if I may, I just wanted to say that in 2008 we did not actually know that the Russians were in violation of the INF Treaty. It took some time to determine that fact. This is an issue that——

Mr. POE. But others of us believed it to be in 2008.

Without arguing over the timeframe, what other options do we have besides withdrawing from the treaty?

Ms. GOTTEMOELLER. I will just say that we will be happy to talk about that matter in closed session, so—but we have a number of options. I have pointed to them already. One has been to, you know, declare countermeasures. That is something we did in the case of the CFE Treaty.

We also, I will say, right at the moment, have a kind of three-pronged approach in place for dealing with this matter. We are continuing to pursue it diplomatically. We have economic counter-measures that we are looking at. And we are also—and my colleague Brian McKeon can talk in more detail about this—we are looking at military measures that we may wish to take.

So we are, in fact, pursuing our own national policy in this regard. And if you are talking about in the realm of legal and treaty work, then we have other options such as countermeasures that can be pursued.

Mr. POE. Is Russia deploying or preparing to deploy tactical nuclear weapons in Crimea?

Ms. GOTTEMOELLER. Sir, I don't know. But we are very, very alert to statements that have been made by certain experts on the Russian side about deploying capable aircraft, dual-capable aircraft, such as backfire and missile systems that would also be dual-capable. And we have spoken to the Russians about this and expressed our concern about any option of reintroducing nuclear weapons into Crimea.

Mr. POE. The Chair will recognize the gentleman from Tennessee, the ranking member, Mr. Cooper.

Mr. COOPER. Thank you, Mr. Chairman.

I want to first thank the witnesses, Ms. Gottemoeller and Mr. McKeon, for their service to the country.

I worry that Congress doesn't make your job any easier. In fact, sometimes it is a nuisance to deal with the legislative branch, but nonetheless we are here.

I think we all agree that the Russians have cheated on this treaty. The question is, what do we do about it?

I am worried, Mr. Chairman, that at least the public portion of this hearing is doing more of a service to the Russians than it is to our own people. It is easy for us to saber-rattle up here and look tough and look strong, but I worry that, you know, authoritarian countries like Russia do not have hearings like this; they do not show their hand. And we should be doing what we can to fight back intelligently, not for domestic political consumption.

Oil, perhaps, might be our most powerful weapon. You know, the ruble has tumbled in recent weeks due to the low oil prices. Most

Americans are rejoicing that oil is, what, about $66 a barrel now. You know, we have some folks in our own country who like high-priced oil. And I am not against our energy-producing regions, but oil as a weapon is a pretty powerful thing. Cheap oil also helps to stabilize Iran, countries like that.

So, somehow or another, we need to figure out what would be the most effective thing. This isn't easy, as I have just pointed out with some geographical disparities within our own country. I am hoping that we as Americans don't get readdicted to foreign oil. We are truly blessed right now to have found so much oil in our own country and to be able to drive oil prices down. I love seeing OPEC in disarray. But we have some folks in our country who love high-priced oil.

So, now, oil is just one of the weapons. There are many others. I actually think the thing that would scare Vladimir Putin the most would be if we lifted defense sequestration. And I look forward to the new Republican majority helping us do that.

In order to do that, we probably are going to have to find either spending cuts, which would be my first choice, or revenue somewhere. And that would be an opportunity to show, for example, that—perhaps the chairman might not be aware, being from the Foreign Affairs Committee, not Defense—that just to maintain our current nuclear stockpile, just maintenance, not improvement, takes $350 billion over the next 10 years. That is a lot of money.

And right now we have difficulty forecasting where that money is going to come from. And for a Nation that didn't even pay for the wars in Iraq and Afghanistan but borrowed much of it from China, that doesn't make us look strong.

So there are opportunities here for America to really be strong and to have an intelligent response to Mr. Putin and others who are warmongering with their violations of the INF Treaty. But let's not beat up on our own diplomats. Let's not beat up on our own Defense Department officials.

You know, sometimes—and I venture to say that each one of us, when you know that your opponent has grievous flaws, as some of us have discovered in our own elections, those aren't necessarily disclosed immediately; sometimes you wait until the final debate— perhaps to give the administration the benefit of the doubt. They thought it was a more strategic opportunity to reveal this and the time was more appropriate.

But we, as Americans, should all be on the same team. We should be unified in our response, an intelligent response, to these treaty violations by Russia. So I would hope, Mr. Chairman, in both the public portion of the hearing and the private portion of the hearing that we can have a first-rate strategic response to these treaty violations.

So thank you, Mr. Chairman. I appreciate your indulgence.

Mr. POE. The Chair recognizes the chairman of the Subcommittee on Strategic Forces, Mr. Rogers.

Mr. ROGERS. Thank you, Mr. Chairman.

Mr. McKeon, what is our strategy for responding to Russia's violation of the INF Treaty? And by that I want to know, what are the ends we are seeking to achieve? And how do we expect to see that happen?

Mr. MCKEON. Mr. Chairman, our strategy has two potential ends.

First, we seek to convince Russia to return to compliance, as Under Secretary Gottemoeller has said, because we believe that preserving the treaty is in our mutual security interests.

If Russia does not return to compliance, our end will be to ensure that Russia gains no significant military advantage from its violation.

Mr. ROGERS. What timeline do you have in mind?

Mr. MCKEON. I can't give you a timeline, sir, as the Under Secretary said. We are taking a hard look at it.

I can say more about this in response to your question, if you will permit me.

Mr. ROGERS. Certainly. I want you to be brief, please. I have some questions for Ms. Gottemoeller.

Mr. MCKEON. Understood.

The ways and means of our strategy address both of these ends. As I said in my statement, we continue to remind Russia why we signed this treaty in the first place. As Rose has said, we have got a range of options—diplomatic, economic, political—that we could impose on Russia that would impose significant costs on them for its violations.

The military responses would aim to negate any advantage Russia might gain from deploying an INF-prohibited system. And all of these would be designed to make us more secure.

The range of options we are looking at in the military sphere fall into three broad categories: Active defenses to counter intermediate-range ground-launched cruise missiles; counterforce capabilities to prevent intermediate-range ground-launched cruise missile attacks; and countervailing strike capabilities to enhance U.S. or allied forces.

Mr. ROGERS. Okay.

Ms. Gottemoeller, has Russia deployed a ground-launched cruise missile violating the INF? Or do they have the capability to do that?

Ms. GOTTEMOELLER. Sir, we have seen them developing a ground-launched cruise missile that is in violation of the INF Treaty. They certainly have the capability to deploy it, we would judge.

Mr. ROGERS. And is there a difference between deployment and this limited operational capability? And describe it for us, please.

Ms. GOTTEMOELLER. Sir, I believe this is something that we might want to take up in more detail in our closed session. We will have some additional assistance from our technical staff at that time.

Mr. ROGERS. Okay.

How many times have you discussed Russia's INF violations with your counterparts since the compliance report came out?

Ms. GOTTEMOELLER. Since the compliance report came out, I would have to count up exactly, but it is in the range of a dozen times.

Mr. ROGERS. To what end?

Ms. GOTTEMOELLER. Well, I will say that the Russians have said quite clearly to us that they believe that the INF Treaty is in their national security interests and that they do not intend to withdraw from the treaty now.

Mr. ROGERS. Do they say why they are not in compliance, then?

Ms. GOTTEMOELLER. They don't acknowledge, sir, that they are not in compliance with the treaty. And that has been one of the core issues that we have had to wrestle with them about at the present time. They say that they are in complete compliance with the INF Treaty.

Mr. ROGERS. And your response?

Ms. GOTTEMOELLER. My response is to repeat to them that we have grave concerns about a ground-launched cruise missile that they have tested to intermediate range. And we have given them some certain key pieces of information to convey to them our understanding of the program. But up to this point, as I said, they have not acknowledged the missile.

Mr. ROGERS. Now, you and Mr. McKeon have stated that you can't state that there is a timeline or you can't tell us what your timeline is. This has got to come to a close soon. Otherwise, the Russians have no reason to believe there are any consequences for violating this treaty or the other seven treaties that they are violating.

Ms. GOTTEMOELLER. Sir, I think we have been really clear with them about the implications of their violation of the treaty. And, in fact, I have said to my counterparts that we do not want to go down the road of putting in place the kind of countermeasures that would, you know, raise the kinds of threats that existed in Europe back at the time that INF was first agreed. And, as Brian McKeon said, we hope the Russians will remember the reasons for which they signed up to the INF Treaty in the first place. It was——

Mr. ROGERS. At any point——

Ms. GOTTEMOELLER [continuing]. To deal with certain threats.

Mr. ROGERS [continuing]. Do you anticipate giving them a drop-dead date?

Ms. GOTTEMOELLER. Sir, that is something that will have to be determined in the context of a discussion, you know, with my bosses. And it will also have to be determined talking with our interagency colleagues.

But I want to really stress that this does not mean that we are doing nothing. We——

Mr. ROGERS. Yes, it does.

Ms. GOTTEMOELLER [continuing]. Are preparing for——

Mr. ROGERS. It really does, Ms. Gottemoeller.

Ms. GOTTEMOELLER. We are preparing for any options here or any possibilities.

Mr. ROGERS. At some point, you have to recognize that there are no consequences when you do nothing. And we are doing nothing. And it has been going on long enough.

I would be much more reassured if you or Mr. McKeon could say, "Yes, sir, they have by December 31, 2015, or it is over," or something. But just to keep saying, we are working on it, you know, we are trying, that could go on forever. And that is one of the reasons they are in Crimea right now.

I am sorry. My time is up.

Mr. POE. The Chair recognizes the gentlelady from California, Ms. Sanchez.

Ms. SANCHEZ. Thank you, Mr. Chairman.

And thank you, both Secretaries, for being before us.

My question is, with respect to the determination of Russia being in noncompliance, why did it take over 2 years to figure that out?

Ms. GOTTEMOELLER. Part of that, ma'am, has to do with the way the interagency process goes forward.

We have a number of inputs that go into that process, one of which, of course, is information that comes from our intelligence agencies and their analyses. Then, in the case of this particular violation, we also had a diplomatic effort going on, again, to try to clarify the matter with the Russian Federation and work with them on it.

And after that process had been going on for some time, then we had our compliance process, which is, again, an interagency activity that puts together the Defense Department, the ICE, the State Department, Energy Department, to look very carefully at all aspects of the situation, because it is a very serious matter to call a country in violation of a treaty.

So that is why it takes some time.

Ms. SANCHEZ. And did the administration, during any of this time, withhold any information from the Congress with respect to this?

Ms. GOTTEMOELLER. No, ma'am. We briefed the Congress regularly throughout this period.

Ms. SANCHEZ. Has Russia responded satisfactorily to the demands that we have made, with respect to the INF compliance?

Ms. GOTTEMOELLER. We have been very concerned, Ms. Sanchez, that, in fact, they have not acknowledged the violation.

Ms. SANCHEZ. They continue to say, there is no violation, we are in compliance. So you are sort of——

Ms. GOTTEMOELLER. Yes.

Ms. SANCHEZ [continuing]. At a standstill with respect to that?

Ms. GOTTEMOELLER. Well, I will put it more succinctly. They have not acknowledged the missile. They have not acknowledged the missile.

Ms. SANCHEZ. Back in the 1980s, how long did it take the USSR to come back into compliance with the ABM Treaty once the USSR had violated that treaty?

Ms. GOTTEMOELLER. The Reagan administration and the Bush administration worked on this. The Soviet Union was declared in noncompliance in 1987. After 5 years of discussion and negotiation, the Russians acknowledged their violation in 1991. Came back into compliance, with the elimination of that radar over the period of time it took to dismantle it, but 1992. So it was a 5-year process.

Ms. SANCHEZ. And, during that time, did the administration continue to engage with the Russians on that issue and others?

Ms. GOTTEMOELLER. Yes, ma'am. During that time, in fact, the Reagan administration negotiated the INF Treaty, and we continued in full compliance with all the treaties and agreements that we had in place at that time, including implementing the SALT II Treaty, which was not ratified at that point but which we had politically agreed to implement with the Soviets.

Ms. SANCHEZ. So, as I recall, when President Reagan submitted the report with respect to noncompliance, he stated that better verification and better compliance provisions would help finding effective ways to ensure compliance is central to the process.

Is this still an ongoing challenge? Should we be investing more in verification? Where is it that we can do a better job so that it is not a 2-year process before we figure out what the heck is going on?

Ms. GOTTEMOELLER. Ma'am, I think the most important thing is national technical means and having very capable national technical means. And this is——

Ms. SANCHEZ. And what does that mean?

Ms. GOTTEMOELLER. That means our own capabilities like satellites, overhead satellites, radar systems, and systems that we have full control of. Of course, it is nice when you have on-site inspection, as we do with New START. That is a very good situation. But, in other treaties and agreements, we do not have on-site inspection. And the on-site inspection regime of the INF Treaty ended in 2001.

So I think that the most important thing is strong investment in our national technical means and preservation of those capabilities and, indeed, expansion of those capabilities.

Ms. SANCHEZ. And, in the current—as you look at the current budgets that we have, are we doing that? Or have we sort of just stepped and expected to be doing this verification and compliance issue with what we have?

Ms. GOTTEMOELLER. Ma'am, again, this area is not wholly in my, you know, budget job jar, so to say. So I think it would make sense to take up this point in our closed session, where we will have a broader group of experts to talk about it.

Ms. SANCHEZ. Thank you. I appreciate your help.

And thank you, Mr. Chairman.

Mr. POE. The Chair recognizes the gentleman from Arizona, Mr. Franks, for 5 minutes.

Mr. FRANKS. Well, thank you, Mr. Chairman.

And thank you both for being here.

Ms. Gottemoeller, I guess I should ask you for some diplomatic immunity here for the rather pointed nature of some of my questions.

You were the key architect for the New START treaty, and, under your negotiation and your arms control expertise, for the first time the United States reduced our strategic nuclear potential while Russia was gaining the opportunity to increase theirs.

And all this time, of course, Russia was cheating on the INF Treaty. And you knew about that, and you didn't say anything. And it really concerns me, in that any negotiations that we have with Iran or any treaty that we have with them, I don't see how, in light of that, that they would have any reticence to cheat on such an agreement.

And now Russia is building a series of first-strike weapons, including its new cruise missile, the submarine, the Severodvinsk class, with the long-range land-attack cruise missile, not to mention its Club-K cruise missile system, and that is one that kind of frightens me significantly. I have a picture of it here, and I wish everyone could take a look at that, where it might be for sale to the right bidder from Russia. And, of course, it is designed to be hidden aboard container cargo ships.

So my question to you is: Why is Russia preparing this variety of first-strike capabilities, and how do these capabilities promote stability?

Ms. GOTTEMOELLER. Sir, if I may right off the bat be straight with you, as well, we did not believe that the Russians were violating the INF Treaty during the period when New START was being negotiated and during the period when it was being considered for ratification, the advice and consent of the Senate for ratification of the treaty. We only became concerned about it later.

Again, this is a topic we can discuss in detail in closed session, and I will be happy to do so, but I did want to be straight with you at the outset about that.

Now, when we negotiated the New START treaty, we realized that, in fact, the Russians were experiencing a mass obsolescence of their Soviet-era systems and that they would be modernizing, as we are now embarking on modernization ourselves. There is a little bit of a phase issue here of modernization programs taking place at different times.

I will stress that one of our concerns in negotiating and putting into place the New START treaty was to ensure that there were certain central limits on what the Russian Federation could deploy.

Mr. FRANKS. But I guess my question to you is, why do you think they are preparing this variety of first-strike capabilities? And how does that contribute to any stability between our countries?

Ms. GOTTEMOELLER. I think partially, sir, it is tradition for the Russian Federation to heavily rely on their ICBM forces. They are a large ground-based power, a large land power, and they have traditionally historically depended on highly accurate ICBM systems. I will say——

Mr. FRANKS. This is more in the area of cruise missiles, I mean, things that are outside our agreement.

Let me shift gears. They are offering this Club-K system at arms sales around the world. I mean, you can find it on the Internet.

And what are the consequences to Russia for selling such systems? And do we have any consequences in mind for them doing that?

Ms. GOTTEMOELLER. We have always been concerned about the sale of high-technology weapons systems freely around the world. We have a whole range of export control regimes that deal with that, some of them multilateral in nature. And we do clearly express our concerns about these kinds of things.

Mr. FRANKS. But given their profound danger, is our response limited to expressing our concerns?

Ms. GOTTEMOELLER. I am not—no, I am not familiar with this particular system and the sales record that the Russians may have had, so we will be prepared to get you more information on that if you are interested.

The last point I wanted to make about their ICBM forces is the central limits of New START really are so small by comparison with the historical numbers that the Russians really do not have the opportunity for a strike capability that would be, you know, a decapitating first strike or something like that. It is just not possible with the lower numbers. And that is why we do emphasize that these kinds of treaties are beneficial for strategic stability.

Mr. FRANKS. As far as their decapitating first-strike capability, that is something we should talk about in the closed session, because there might be some issues to take on that front.

Mr. McKeon, if I could, to try to squeeze it in under my time here, how is DoD responding to the rise in Russian first-strike capability development and planning?

Mr. MCKEON. If I could, sir, briefly on the Club-K, I am no expert on it, and we will get you more information, but I don't believe they have sold it yet. They have been showing it off at arms shows——

Mr. FRANKS. Just the arms shows, yeah.

Mr. MCKEON. Yes.

Mr. FRANKS. But it doesn't encourage me that——

Mr. MCKEON. No, it is not a great sign. I am not trying to downplay the concern that you have. I just don't think it has been sold yet to—they are marketing it at arms shows.

As I said, sir, earlier in response to Chairman Rogers, we are looking at a number of possible countermeasures in the military sphere, ranging from reactive defense to counterforce to countervailing defense measures. I don't want to get into the specifics because we are still working through various options, but we have a broad range of options, some of which would be compliant with the INF Treaty, some of which would not be, that we would be able to recommend to our leadership if a decision were taken to go down that path.

Mr. FRANKS. Well, thank you, Mr. Chairman.

Mr. POE. The Chair recognizes the ranking member of the TNT committee, Mr. Sherman from California.

Mr. SHERMAN. Thank you.

What are the military benefits to the Russians of the violations we are accusing them of? If they developed and deployed these intermediate-range missiles, would that enhance their ability to threaten our European allies? Or do they already have enough ICBMs to deal with both whatever they would want to do off the European continent but also on the European continent, as well?

Ms. GOTTEMOELLER. Sir, it has been a fact from the outset that an ICBM, an intermediate-range target could be handled by an intercontinental-range system. That is just a fact——

Mr. SHERMAN. Right.

Ms. GOTTEMOELLER [continuing]. That has been well understood, in fact, since the INF Treaty and before. So our view is that the Russians have adequate capability to handle issues around their periphery.

They actually argue, again, among their expert community that the targets in Eurasia are the ones that concern them most, not necessarily emphasis on NATO and the European allies but targets across Asia, as well.

But this is a good question for the Russians, because it is not—you know, we don't see a need for the system, quite honestly.

Mr. SHERMAN. So they are spending a lot of money at what now is tough economic times for them to develop, in violation of their treaty obligations, a basically duplicative system that will allow them to do that which their ICBMs could already do in both Europe and Asia.

Ms. GOTTEMOELLER. Yes, sir. That is our point of view.

Mr. SHERMAN. Now, the treaty provides for a special Intermediate-Range Nuclear Forces Treaty Special Verification Commission. Have we invoked that formal provision, and do we plan to?

Ms. GOTTEMOELLER. Sir, we wanted to drive this issue to a higher level, and, in fact, I believe since I briefed this group the last time, we have had President Obama writing to President Putin. We have also had my boss, Secretary Kerry, but also Secretary Hagel and Chairman Dempsey all speaking to their counterparts at a high level about our grave concern in this matter, as well as I continue my diplomacy in this arena.

So we really wanted to drive it to a high level and not have it being handled in the more or less routine channels of the SVC.

Mr. SHERMAN. So we haven't convened this special commission because we wanted to do something even more formal and more powerful.

Ms. GOTTEMOELLER. Correct, sir. That is the idea, to have a very, very strong spotlight shown on the measures, on the issue.

Mr. SHERMAN. What does Russia get from this treaty? They claim we violate it. They themselves are violating it. We pulled out of the ABM Treaty. They could solve a lot of diplomatic problems by just pulling out of this treaty. What benefit do they get from our compliance with the treaty?

Ms. GOTTEMOELLER. I think it is the same benefit, sir, that they got when they signed up to the treaty back in the late 1980s—that is, this treaty, by banning the deployment of intermediate-range nuclear systems, addresses the treat of a short-warning, very short-warning attack on critical strategic targets such as strategic command and control. So the benefits to the Russians are the same as they always were in terms of the military benefits.

Mr. SHERMAN. And from that standpoint, they benefit more than we do. Since the days of missiles in Cuba, the Russians have never been able to use that short-range, short-warning against us. And yet, if this treaty were to fall apart, NATO would have that capacity against their most sensitive assets, correct?

Ms. GOTTEMOELLER. Well, sir, I don't want to jump out ahead of my DoD colleagues in terms of what precisely would be the countermeasures. Mr. McKeon might want to talk to that. But——

Mr. SHERMAN. Why don't we ask him to——

Ms. GOTTEMOELLER [continuing]. If I may, I just want to stress that we are talking about here ground-launched cruise missiles in this case, and I think that is the important thing. The Russians have sea-based capabilities and air-based capabilities that can also threaten CONUS, of course.

Mr. SHERMAN. Mr. McKeon?

Mr. MCKEON. Sir, we don't have ground-launched cruise missiles in Europe now, obviously, because they are prohibited by the treaty, but that would obviously be one option to explore, some kind of——

Mr. SHERMAN. Yeah. The point I was making is I think Russia has more to lose if this treaty falls apart than we do because we have land-based facilities within between 500 kilometers and 5,500 kilometers of their most sensitive sites; they do not have land bases within that range of our sites.

And, with that, I will yield back.

Mr. Poe. The gentleman yields back his time.

The Chair recognizes the gentleman from Ohio, Mr. Turner, for 5 minutes.

Mr. Turner. Thank you, Mr. Chairman.

Thank you both for being here.

I want to disagree first, Mr. McKeon, with a comment you made. You said that arms control is the most important tool we have for national security. I just want to put a footnote to that: Of course, China, North Korea, Iran, Pakistan have not been part of the reduction of the nuclear threat to the United States.

Ms. Gottemoeller, you very frequently in your testimony here said, ''That would be best answered in closed session.'' Well, let me just tell you, as I begin to ask you these questions, that will not be an acceptable answer to my questions. I have sat here, and there is not one person that has asked you anything that is classified that you can't answer. And although you may choose it would be best to answer it in closed session, this is an open session, the questions we ask are open, and they are questions that you have responsibility to answer for both the American public and to Congress. So I will not be accepting that the best answer would be in closed session. I accept your best answer here.

We are going to return back to the issue of Russia violating or not being clearly in compliance with its treaties. Chairman Poe had asked if it was not in compliance with as many as eight. You identified that they were not in compliance with the Treaty on Intermediate-Range Nuclear Forces, the INF, and that they were not in compliance with the Treaty on Conventional Armed Forces in Europe, CFE. That is two.

You then said to him that there were others, but you didn't specify what those others—and it doesn't require closed session for you to specify those because it is not classified. So I would like to ask you, in what others is Russia violating or not clearly in compliance besides those two?

Ms. Gottemoeller. We have long been concerned about their Soviet-era programs of chemical weapons and biological weapons. And so we have continued to express great concern about those——

Mr. Turner. So is Russia violating or not clearly in compliance with the Biological Weapons Convention, BWC, or the Chemical Weapons Convention, CWC? Your answer is?

Ms. Gottemoeller. We are continuing to press them on providing us information about those two——

Mr. Turner. Are they——

Ms. Gottemoeller [continuing]. Programs.

Mr. Turner [continuing]. In compliance with those two treaties?

You know the answer. Provide the answer. It is not classified. If you have concerns—you either can or cannot testify before us that they are in compliance.

Are they in compliance with the Biological Weapons Convention, BWC? Yes or no? Yes or no? Not classified. Clearly within your realm. Clearly within something that is public consumption and certainly is something for oversight for Congress. Are they in compliance with the Biological Weapons Convention, your scope of your employment, BWC? Are they?

Ms. GOTTEMOELLER. With regard to the Soviet-era programs, no——

Mr. TURNER. Great. Okay.

Ms. GOTTEMOELLER [continuing]. We have problems.

Mr. TURNER. So we have three from you now.

The next one that you mentioned was the Chemical Weapons Convention, CWC. Are they in compliance with the Chemical Weapons Convention, CWC? Yes or no?

Ms. GOTTEMOELLER. With regard to the Soviet-era programs, no, but——

Mr. TURNER. Okay. So that is four.

Ms. GOTTEMOELLER [continuing]. Sir, if I may——

Mr. TURNER. We are clicking along here. New START Treaty, are they in compliance or not in compliance?

Ms. GOTTEMOELLER. Yes.

Mr. TURNER. Yes what?

Ms. GOTTEMOELLER. Yes, they are in compliance.

Mr. TURNER. Okay. Great. Thanks.

Okay. Let's see—nope, that is an acronym. The Treaty on Open Skies, compliance or not in compliance?

Ms. GOTTEMOELLER. They are in compliance with the Open Skies Treaty, sir.

Mr. TURNER. The moratorium on nuclear testing, are they in compliance or not in compliance, Ms. Gottemoeller?

Ms. GOTTEMOELLER. The moratorium on nuclear testing, yes, we believe they are in compliance with their moratorium. But you do realize, sir, that this is not a legally binding treaty. It is, you know—essentially, it is a political——

Mr. TURNER. It is one within the realm of responsibility of your employment, is it not?

Ms. GOTTEMOELLER. Correct.

Mr. TURNER. Great. That is why I wanted an answer from you. The Vienna Convention?

Ms. GOTTEMOELLER. The Vienna Document, sir?

Mr. TURNER. Compliance or not compliance?

Ms. GOTTEMOELLER. They are in compliance with the Vienna Document.

Again, these are politically binding commitments. They are confidence-building measures. And, again, we have some concerns with how they have implemented certain aspects of the Vienna Document.

Mr. TURNER. But your concerns are not that they are violating it?

Ms. GOTTEMOELLER. Our concern is that they are not——

Mr. TURNER. It would have to be they are violating it, right? I mean, you don't have concerns that maybe they are just, you know, not fully committed to it. It is either they are complying or not complying. You have concerns as to whether or not they are not complying, right?

Ms. GOTTEMOELLER. Correct. We——

Mr. TURNER. Great.

Ms. GOTTEMOELLER. Okay.

Mr. TURNER. So we will count that in the category of "maybe."

The Missile Technology Control Regime, MTCR, compliance or not compliance?

Ms. GOTTEMOELLER. The Missile Technology Control Regime we believe that they are essentially in compliance with, but I will say that, again——

Mr. TURNER. The Budapest Memorandum? I think we can both kind of guess what your answer should be on that one.

Ms. GOTTEMOELLER. I definitely agree with you on that one, sir.

Mr. TURNER. And that would be?

Ms. GOTTEMOELLER. They are not in compliance with——

Mr. TURNER. Great.

Ms. GOTTEMOELLER [continuing]. The Budapest Memorandum.

Mr. TURNER. All right.

Ms. GOTTEMOELLER. But, again, let me stress that this is a political——

Mr. TURNER. All right. One, two, three, four, five. Okay, so there are five, at least, you would tell us openly that they are violating.

When you said to Chairman Poe that there were others, are there others besides the Treaty on Intermediate-Range Nuclear Forces, INF; the Biological Weapons Convention, BWC; the Chemical Weapons Convention, CWC; the Treaty on Conventional Armed Forces in Europe, CFE; the Budapest Memorandum that you believe they are violating?

Ms. GOTTEMOELLER. No.

Mr. TURNER. Are there others?

Ms. GOTTEMOELLER. I do not, sir.

Mr. TURNER. So you say there are no others?

Ms. GOTTEMOELLER. I do not at the moment recall any others.

Mr. TURNER. "Do not recall." I mean, this is your professional responsibility to recall. This is not like, you know, Mr. Gruber coming here and saying, "I just suddenly don't remember what I was talking about." I mean, this is your responsibility.

Are there others, or are there not?

Ms. GOTTEMOELLER. No, sir, there are none others that I know of.

Mr. TURNER. Thank you, Mr. Chairman. I yield back.

Mr. POE. The Chair recognizes the gentleman from Rhode Island, Mr. Langevin, for 5 minutes.

Mr. LANGEVIN. Thank you, Mr. Chairman.

To our witnesses, in particular Deputy Under Secretary McKeon, what are the risks for national security if the U.S. withdraws from the INF or from New START as a response to Russian INF violations?

Mr. MCKEON. Well, in terms of the INF Treaty, sir, the primary risk is greater instability in Europe if the Russians were to deploy this noncompliance system in significant numbers.

In terms of withdrawal from New START, right now there are central limits under the treaty on strategic systems. They come into effect in early 2018 and then last for 3 years after that. So if we were to withdraw from the treaty, there would be no limitations on Russian strategic systems and we would lose the verification regime of that treaty, including the on-site inspections.

So, over time, we would continue to have less and less knowledge of Russian strategic systems, which would make the Joint Chiefs nervous, and there would be no limitations on their strategic systems, which we don't think would be to our benefit.

Mr. LANGEVIN. So, in your assessment, does arms control support national security? And if so, how?

Mr. MCKEON. Yes, sir, it does. And I believe in my statement I said it is an important element, not the most important element, of national security.

Mr. LANGEVIN. Under Secretary Gottemoeller, why did the U.S. not simply withdraw from the ABM Treaty in the 1980s?

Ms. GOTTEMOELLER. As I understood, sir, there was a view at the time, again, that it contributed to strategic stability, and there was, I think, a good record of discussions on what was going on with the Krasnoyarsk radar at that time. But the treaty was seen as being important to the balance between strategic offensive and defensive forces at that time.

Mr. LANGEVIN. Was diplomacy successful in that instance? And how?

Ms. GOTTEMOELLER. In the end, yes, diplomacy was successful. It was a long and difficult discussion with the Soviet Union to begin with and then the Russian Federation, but the Russian Federation did end up dismantling the Krasnoyarsk radar and returning to full compliance with the ABM Treaty.

Mr. LANGEVIN. Given the what appear to be significant violations of the INF Treaty, should the U.S. withdraw from INF?

Ms. GOTTEMOELLER. My view, sir, is that we should not in any way take steps that would essentially give the Russians a bye in this matter. If we withdrew from the INF Treaty, it would legalize the illegal actions they are taking now, and I don't think that is in our interest to do so.

Mr. LANGEVIN. All right.

Under Secretary Gottemoeller, Secretary McKeon, the Defense Science Board concluded in a January 2014 report that, I quote, ''monitoring for proliferation should be a top national security objective but one for which the Nation is not yet organized or fully equipped.''

Do you agree? And what are State and DoD doing to address this deficiency?

Ms. GOTTEMOELLER. Sir, perhaps I will allow Mr. McKeon to answer that. I gave my version of views on that to Mrs. Sanchez.

So, Brian, would you like to add anything?

Mr. MCKEON. Sir, I am not familiar with that particular report. I think, as a general matter, we would agree that we can make more investments in verification technologies. And you will have some folks from the IC in the closed session, and they could probably speak with a little more detail about some of their deficiencies and investments we ought to be making.

Mr. LANGEVIN. Okay.

Since I still have some time, Secretary Gottemoeller, in answering some of the previous questions of my colleague on Russia's compliance or noncompliance on several treaties, you weren't fully able to finish your answers. Do you want to add to that and complete your answers where you weren't fully able to do so?

Ms. GOTTEMOELLER. Thank you, sir.

I think the important point is that there are two treaties, the INF Treaty and the CFE Treaty, where we are fully concerned about violation of the treaty by the Russian Federation.

In some of the areas we were discussing, like the Chemical Weapons Convention, I always like to stress that we don't want to throw out the baby with the bathwater. The Russians continue to eliminate their Soviet-era holdings, and I just gave a speech in The Hague last week noting the intensified efforts by the Russians to get rid of their chemical weapons from the Soviet era.

So, although we have concerns about the Soviet-era programs and that they haven't given us all the data that they may have with regard to those programs, we are satisfied that they are intensively working to eliminate the huge stock of chemical weapons that they have from that era.

Mr. LANGEVIN. Very good. My time has expired, but thank you. And I yield back.

Mr. POE. The gentleman yields back his time.

The Chair recognizes the gentleman from Ohio, Mr. Lamborn.

Mr. LAMBORN. Colorado.

Mr. POE. Colorado. I am sorry. Did I insult Colorado or Ohio?

Mr. LAMBORN. No, they are both great States.

Mr. McKeon, is Russia deploying or preparing to deploy tactical nuclear weapons in Crimea?

Mr. McKEON. Sir, I don't know the answer to that. We have not seen that, but we are watching it closely.

Mr. LAMBORN. Are there not open-source reports that such is the case?

Mr. McKEON. We have seen some of those open-source reports, but I don't think we have seen—and we could get into it in the closed session—I don't think we have seen that actually occurring.

Mr. LAMBORN. Okay. Well, maybe we can talk more about that later.

Ms. Gottemoeller, what is the position of the Department of State concerning a moratorium on testing of kinetic energy antisatellite weapons?

Ms. GOTTEMOELLER. Sir, we have looked at that option as a perhaps diplomatic option that we would like to pursue, but we are not placing any emphasis on it at this time.

Mr. LAMBORN. Okay. I might come back to you in a second on this. I want to see what DoD thinks about that.

Mr. McKeon, does DoD have a position on such an action that we just discussed?

Mr. McKEON. I apologize, sir. I was consulting my colleagues on another issue, and I didn't hear your question.

Mr. LAMBORN. Okay. Anything concerning a moratorium, with our country and any others, on not testing, so as not to test, kinetic energy antisatellite weapons or methods?

Mr. McKEON. I will confess I am only in the Department 4 months. I don't believe we are pursing or considering a moratorium of that kind.

Mr. LAMBORN. Okay.

My concern is that there may have been discussion about that by some folks in the Department of State that was done unilaterally without talking to DoD, because DoD would be, I think, less receptive to such a thing, knowing more about what is really at stake.

Mr. McKeon. Sir, it is a big government, and there are lots of people and lots of layers, and there may be people in different departments who have talked about it, but I don't believe that is the position of the United States Government at this time.

Mr. Lamborn. Okay.

And back to you, that is not a U.S. Government position?

Ms. Gottemoeller. That is correct, sir.

And I did want to emphasize, I mentioned a moment ago that there had been some discussions and consideration of it, and these were fully interagency discussions. I do want to underscore that there were opportunities to fully discuss and consider pros and cons and so forth on an interagency basis. And so there shouldn't be a sense that this was, you know, something that was being pursued unilaterally by the U.S. Department of State.

But, as I said, we are not placing an emphasis on pursuing it at this time.

Mr. Lamborn. Well, good, because I would be very concerned if Department of State was pursuing something without talking to the folks at Department of Defense.

Ms. Gottemoeller. Sir, my experience is that simply doesn't work.

Mr. Lamborn. Okay. We are all in agreement on that.

Mr. McKeon. Yeah. Sir, if I might add, I will speak to my own newness in the Department, and I have certainly not heard any discussion of this issue. I didn't mean to say that——

Mr. Lamborn. Okay.

Mr. McKeon [continuing]. People in State were not coordinating with DoD. I just have not——

Mr. Lamborn. Okay.

Mr. McKeon [continuing]. Seen that in my short time.

Mr. Lamborn. Okay. Thank you for that.

Now, changing subjects, if I am not mistaken, Ms. Gottemoeller, you said earlier that INF weapons that the Russians would be pursuing in violation of the INF, you know, cruise missiles between 500 and 5,000 kilometers——

Ms. Gottemoeller. Uh-huh.

Mr. Lamborn [continuing]. Would be only duplicative of what they already have a capability of doing with strategic missiles. Is that——

Ms. Gottemoeller. That is our understanding, sir, and our view as to why this is a redundant kind of capability.

Mr. Lamborn. Well, with that in mind, that seems to contradict what General Breedlove has said, the commander of our European forces. In an April news report, he said, "A weapons capability that violates the INF that is introduced into the greater European landmass is absolutely a tool that will have to be dealt with. It can't go unanswered."

Ms. Gottemoeller. I agree with that, sir, absolutely, particularly in the context that this is a weapon that has been banned for, you know, decades at this point. There are many reasons on the political and the military front that we must respond to it.

Mr. LAMBORN. So when you use the word "duplicative," you are not in any way slighting that capability, which someone might assume. You are saying this is a very serious matter.

Ms. GOTTEMOELLER. Absolutely.

Mr. LAMBORN. Okay. Because "duplicative" means, oh, is it really that big of a deal?

Ms. GOTTEMOELLER. Well, again, my colleague from the Defense Department may wish to speak to this, but the only point I was saying is that we have known from the time that the ban was put in place in the late 1980s that if a country wished to use an ICBM, an intermediate-range system, in a depressed trajectory or a lofted trajectory, it could do so, and it would have the same kind of potential against intermediate-range targets in that kind of use.

Mr. LAMBORN. And, lastly, you do agree with General Breedlove, this must be dealt with?

Ms. GOTTEMOELLER. Absolutely, sir. Yes.

Mr. LAMBORN. Thank you very much.

Mr. Chairman, I yield back.

Mr. POE. The Chair recognizes the gentleman from California, Mr. Garamendi, for 5 minutes.

Mr. GARAMENDI. I thank you, Mr. Chairman.

Secretary Gottemoeller, you were asked a series of questions about the various treaties and agreements, and you were compelled to answer "yes" or "no," which is usually a way we use to try to trap people.

Would you please, for the record, provide the additional information that this committee needs to fully understand the answers to your question?

Ms. GOTTEMOELLER. Yes, sir. I will be happy to do that. Thank you for the opportunity.

Mr. GARAMENDI. I think he went through seven or maybe eight different treaties and agreements. I am sure the record would help you remember all of them.

I personally dislike that kind of activity because it does not fully inform us about some very complex matters. I will take that up with Mr. Turner when I have him outside this room. And I wish he were here. It is just something we shouldn't be doing. We should get full answers if we really want to understand.

I do have a series of questions. I suspect most of them are going to have to come in a closed session. But a lot of this is more about Europe than it is about the United States. What is the NATO position on all of these matters?

Ms. GOTTEMOELLER. I will begin. Perhaps my colleague would like to comment, as well.

Our NATO allies have been very, very committed to arms control treaties and agreements as a way to enhance security and stability not only in Europe but also beyond. And they count on our leadership in trying to develop and continue to strengthen these regimes.

And so we have briefed them regularly on our very grave concern with regard to Russian noncompliance in this case. They have been very concerned about it, but they have been very supportive of our efforts to bring the Russians back into compliance with the treaty.

Mr. GARAMENDI. Are they suggesting that we bail out of the treaty?

Ms. GOTTEMOELLER. By no means, sir. Quite the opposite. They are very keen to ensure that we work in every way we can to bring Russia back into compliance with the treaty.

Mr. GARAMENDI. Mr. McKeon, is that the view of the Department of Defense also?

Mr. MCKEON. It is, sir.

And what I might add is that, although the NATO states are not parties to the treaty—it was originally a treaty between us and the USSR and now the successor states of the USSR—they are great beneficiaries of the treaty. So they are quite interested in it remaining in force.

And, as the Under Secretary has said, we have kept them extensively briefed. After we went to Moscow in September, she briefed them by videoconference, the North Atlantic Council, on our efforts. And we have been working with them on their own intelligence and military assessment.

Mr. GARAMENDI. Okay.

I think you may have answered this once before, but does the Department of Defense hold the position that we should remain with the INF Treaty?

Mr. MCKEON. It is the position of the Department and of the administration that we should continue to be in the treaty and seek to bring the Russians back into compliance at this time. But we are planning for other options to push them back into the treaty or if the day should come that we don't want to be in the treaty any longer.

But, yes, for the time being, it is the position of the administration we should stay in the treaty.

Mr. GARAMENDI. Okay. It is my understanding that the principal issue is the delivery system or systems. Is that correct?

Mr. MCKEON. That is correct.

Mr. GARAMENDI. Okay. Are they attempting to develop a new nuclear weapon or enhance an existing nuclear weapon?

Mr. MCKEON. I think we should save that for the closed session, sir.

Mr. GARAMENDI. I had expected that answer.

I think I will yield back at this point and await a closed session.

Mr. POE. I thank the gentleman from California.

The Chair recognizes the gentleman from Pennsylvania, Mr. Perry, for 5 minutes.

Mr. PERRY. Thank you, Mr. Chairman.

Ladies and gentlemen, thank you for your service to the country.

Ms. Gottemoeller, is there a difference in our ability to detect an ICBM versus a GLCM?

Ms. GOTTEMOELLER. Sir, they are different kinds of systems. An intercontinental ballistic missile——

Mr. PERRY. I know what they are. I am just asking——

Ms. GOTTEMOELLER. Yeah.

Mr. PERRY. So isn't there a strategic advantage then, wouldn't Russia have a strategic advantage to have that delivery system that was undetectable by us because it—you know, it runs across the ground. I mean, by the time you see it, it is past you. Isn't that a strategic capability?

Ms. GOTTEMOELLER. I would say that it offers some, you know, capability to the Russians. Clearly, they have not had intermediate-range systems up to this point.

Mr. PERRY. Some? It offers a lot. We can't do anything about it. Once it is launched——

Ms. GOTTEMOELLER. But they have had a number of very capable both air-breathing systems, cruise missile systems, and intercontinental—the ballistic system——

Mr. PERRY. Right.

Ms. GOTTEMOELLER [continuing]. For many, many years now. And so, in terms of the increment of new capability, that is, I think, what we have to be concerned about.

Mr. PERRY. Right. This is a big step.

Ma'am, I heard you say earlier that we hoped that they weren't going to embark on this. And with all due respect, I see this as, you know, they hope—or we hope—we hoped they wouldn't go into Ukraine, and we hoped they wouldn't shut off the gas valve, and we hoped a lot of things, but they took action, and we continue to hope.

And another thing you said, that they didn't acknowledge the violation. Do we require them to acknowledge the violation before we act? I mean, if you are lying about something—like, right now they are saying, "We are not in Ukraine." Do we require them to acknowledge the violation? Is that——

Ms. GOTTEMOELLER. Well, sir, I worked with them for over a year in the diplomatic realm to really see what we could do in the diplomatic realm to get them back into treaty compliance before we declared them in noncompliance last July, before we declared this violation.

Mr. PERRY. Right.

Ms. GOTTEMOELLER. So we do, of course, do everything that we need to do——

Mr. PERRY. I understand we do everything——

Ms. GOTTEMOELLER. We do everything that we need to do, including working on the diplomatic, economic, and military front, to put in place the policies that we need to have to counter this violation.

Mr. PERRY. And I would agree with you that diplomacy is preferable. But timing and the time that it takes also is a factor here, because other things are occurring while we are talking, and that is a concern.

And I am concerned that we are counting on them to be the good actors, when they have a storied and longstanding history of violating and lying and obfuscating. And it concerns me that we just continue to go on.

That having been said, do you believe that further unilateral disarmament by the United States is a correct response at any level?

Ms. GOTTEMOELLER. Sir, such unilateral reductions are not on the table.

Mr. PERRY. Okay. But we have heard that the President has discussed that, is considering that, might consider that, and I just want you on the record. You would agree that that is not an appropriate response at this time?

Ms. GOTTEMOELLER. As I said, sir, they are not on the table.

44

Mr. PERRY. Okay. And you agree that it is not a correct response?

Ms. GOTTEMOELLER. Sir, you know that I have people above my pay grade——

Mr. PERRY. Sure. But I am asking you. I get it. I am asking you, as the subject-matter expert that the Nation is depending on, you, what is your response?

Ms. GOTTEMOELLER. Sir, I am happy to tell you that such unilateral reductions are not on the table, and I think that is the correct——

Mr. PERRY. Okay. So you are not——

Ms. GOTTEMOELLER [continuing]. Response.

Mr. PERRY. I understand. You are not going to answer.

Do you believe that the U.S. has violated our obligations regarding any of these agreements that have so far been stated, seven or eight of them? Have we materially violated any of them? I know Russia accuses us. They accuse a lot of things. But do you believe we have violated any of them?

Ms. GOTTEMOELLER. Sir, if you take a look at our compliance report, we determined that we are in full compliance with all of the treaties and agreements.

Mr. PERRY. Okay. So is America safer and more secure if we abide by the treaty and Russia continues to cheat?

Ms. GOTTEMOELLER. I think the important word here, sir, is "vigilance," that we have to recognize when there are problems in compliance, when there are actual violations, we have to be very vigilant and we have to deal with them. We cannot be taken by surprise. But I think, in general, yes, they continue to provide for mutual stability, predictability, and security.

Mr. PERRY. With all due respect—and I agree that vigilance is important, diplomacy is important. But we are talking about nuclear weapons being placed around places that are of vital interest to the United States and the world, and there is no margin for error.

With that in mind, what would you suggest is the appropriate role for Congress in responding to this situation, as it appears that the administration cannot or will not respond timely?

Ms. GOTTEMOELLER. Well, sir, I would say that the importance of your oversight can never be overstated. We have an open——

Mr. PERRY. We understand the importance, but what——

Ms. GOTTEMOELLER. We have an open hearing here today.

Mr. PERRY. What would you suggest would be our correct response to safeguard our Nation and the world in our treaty obligations?

Ms. GOTTEMOELLER. Well, sir, I do want to emphasize that we do take action in this matter, we have taken action in this matter, and we will continue to take action in this matter. And we appreciate your partnership in supporting our efforts.

Mr. PERRY. Mr. Chairman, I yield back.

Mr. POE. I thank the gentleman.

The Chair recognizes the gentleman from Oklahoma, Mr. Bridenstine, for 5 minutes.

Mr. BRIDENSTINE. Thank you, Mr. Chairman.

And I would like to thank the gentleman from Pennsylvania. I think he is hitting on a critically important point about imposing unilateral commitments on ourselves.

And it opens up, I think, an important philosophical question for you, Mrs. Gottemoeller. If we were to comply with the INF and they were to continue violating the INF, do we have a treaty at all?

Ms. GOTTEMOELLER. I think one thing that is important to recall, sir, is that there are a number of countries who are parties to this treaty, 11 countries in addition to the Russian Federation and the United States. And so it is an entire treaty system that extends across Eurasia.

So I think in our efforts—and I mentioned this earlier—it is very important to continue to press the Russians to come back into compliance with the treaty. If somehow we left the treaty, then it would essentially be giving them a free ride to do whatever they well pleased. So I think it is important to say that they are in violation, that there is a problem, you know, they are not abiding by their treaty commitments, and not give them a free ride.

Mr. BRIDENSTINE. So if we were to pull out of the INF, earlier you mentioned that that would make legal their illegal actions; is that correct?

Ms. GOTTEMOELLER. Correct.

Mr. BRIDENSTINE. So currently they are in violation of the law.

Ms. GOTTEMOELLER. Correct.

Mr. BRIDENSTINE. And that is going to supposedly encourage them to get back in compliance with the law.

Ms. GOTTEMOELLER. I think if international law means anything to the Russian Federation, they should be considering that matter.

Mr. BRIDENSTINE. What did international law have to say about the invasion and occupation of South Ossetia, for example?

Ms. GOTTEMOELLER. Well, I said in the outset of my remarks, of my testimony——

Mr. BRIDENSTINE. Real quick, what did——

Ms. GOTTEMOELLER [continuing]. That we are gravely concerned about——

Mr. BRIDENSTINE. What did international law say about the invasion and occupation of Abkhazia?

Ms. GOTTEMOELLER. We are very concerned about——

Mr. BRIDENSTINE. What did international law say about the invasion and occupation of Crimea?

Ms. GOTTEMOELLER. We are very concerned——

Mr. BRIDENSTINE. At what point——

Ms. GOTTEMOELLER [continuing]. About all those matters.

Mr. BRIDENSTINE. At what point does the international law mean anything as long as we continue to allow them to violate international law?

Ms. GOTTEMOELLER. I think, sir, that the important thing is that the structure of international law provides for global security and stability overall. And because there are violations out there—and in the case of Crimea, you pointed to this very strong example, you know, on the current scene, that Russia has violated the territorial integrity and sovereignty of Ukraine by coming into Crimea and by, you know, bringing their troops into eastern Ukraine, as well.

But that doesn't mean, you know, that we do away with the OSCE principles or the U.N. charter. The system of law, it is important to maintain it in place——

Mr. BRIDENSTINE. So do you personally believe——

Ms. GOTTEMOELLER [continuing]. As a way to go after countries that then violate.

Mr. BRIDENSTINE. Let's say we have a bilateral commitment with Russia, a bilateral commitment, and they are in violation, the question is, do we continue to impose unilateral commitment upon ourselves that hinder us but enable them to continue to progress?

Ms. GOTTEMOELLER. I think the important thing, sir——

Mr. BRIDENSTINE. Just "yes" or "no," do you think we should do that? Philosophically, do you think we should impose commitments upon ourself that hinder our ability while they are continuing to progress?

Ms. GOTTEMOELLER. In this case, the answer is "yes" to stay within the treaty and then to look at what countermeasures we have available—Mr. McKeon already mentioned we have a number of military countermeasures—that stay within the realm of the treaty.

Mr. BRIDENSTINE. Okay.

So I have 1½ minutes left. Mr. McKeon, we are talking about cruise missiles here. What type of ability do we have as a Nation militarily to provide early warning to our friends and allies in Europe that these missiles may be engaged?

Mr. McKEON. Sir, we could talk in more detail in closed session about our military capabilities in Europe. I don't want to advertise for the Russians what capabilities we have in Europe.

Obviously, with short- or intermediate-range missiles closer to Europe's and NATO's borders, it leads to shorter warning time, and you have to have adequate sensors to have point defense.

So we have some capabilities. I don't want to overstate what those are.

Mr. PERRY. And then, as far as the ability to hold at risk targets, do we have that ability?

Mr. McKEON. Yes.

Mr. BRIDENSTINE. Roger that.

I yield back.

Mr. POE. I thank the gentleman.

This concludes the open session of these two subcommittees. The subcommittees will recess to 2212 for a classified briefing, and we will continue in 10 minutes, 4:05, as the clock on the courtroom wall, to quote a phrase.

[Whereupon, at 3:55 p.m., the subcommittees recessed, to reconvene in closed session at 4:05 p.m. the same day.]

APPENDIX

MATERIAL SUBMITTED FOR THE RECORD

JOINT SUBCOMMITTEE HEARING NOTICE
COMMITTEE ON FOREIGN AFFAIRS
COMMITTEE ON ARMED SERVICES
U.S. HOUSE OF REPRESENTATIVES
WASHINGTON, DC 20515-6128

Subcommittee on Terrorism, Nonproliferation, and Trade
Ted Poe (R-TX), Chairman

Subcommittee on Strategic Forces
Mike Rogers (R-AL), Chairman

TO: MEMBERS OF THE COMMITTEE ON FOREIGN AFFAIRS

You are respectfully requested to attend an OPEN hearing of the Committee on Foreign Affairs, to be held jointly by the Subcommittee on Terrorism, Nonproliferation, and Trade and the Subcommittee on Strategic Forces in Room 2118 of the Rayburn House Office Building (and available live on the Committee website at http://www.ForeignAffairs.house.gov):

DATE: Wednesday, December 10, 2014

TIME: 2:00 p.m.

SUBJECT: Russian Arms Control Cheating and the Administration's Responses

WITNESSES: The Honorable Rose Gottemoeller
Under Secretary for Arms Control and International Security
U.S. Department of State

The Honorable Brian McKeon
Principal Deputy Under Secretary for Policy
U.S. Department of Defense

By Direction of the Chairman

The Committee on Foreign Affairs seeks to make its facilities accessible to persons with disabilities. If you are in need of special accommodations, please call 202/225-5021 at least four business days in advance of the event, whenever practicable. Questions with regard to special accommodations in general (including availability of Committee materials in alternative formats and assistive listening devices) may be directed to the Committee.

COMMITTEE ON FOREIGN AFFAIRS

MINUTES OF SUBCOMMITTEE ON _HFAC Terrorism Nonproliferation and Trade; HASC Strategic Forces_ HEARING

Day___*Wednesday*___Date___*December 10, 2014*___Room_____*2118*_____

Starting Time _____*2:01 p.m.*_____ Ending Time ___*3:55 p.m.*___

Recesses ___*1*___ (*2:13* to *2:51*) (____to____) (____to____) (____to____) (____to____) (____to____)

Presiding Member(s)

Chairman Ted Poe

Check all of the following that apply:

Open Session ☑   Electronically Recorded (taped) ☑
Executive (closed) Session ☐   Stenographic Record ☑
Televised ☑

TITLE OF HEARING:

"Russian Arms Control Cheating and the Administration's Responses"

SUBCOMMITTEE MEMBERS PRESENT:

Reps. Poe, Rogers, Franks, Turner, Lamborn, Coffman, Kinzinger, Bridenstine, Perry, Sherman, Cooper, Sanchez, Langevin, Garamendi, and Veasey

NON-SUBCOMMITTEE MEMBERS PRESENT: *(Mark with an * if they are not members of full committee.)*

HEARING WITNESSES: Same as meeting notice attached? Yes ☑ No ☐
(If "no", please list below and include title, agency, department, or organization.)

STATEMENTS FOR THE RECORD: *(List any statements submitted for the record.)*

QFRs Submitted by Reps. Garamendi, Turner, Rogers, and Cooper

TIME SCHEDULED TO RECONVENE_____
or
TIME ADJOURNED ___*4:24 p.m.*___

_____
Subcommittee Staff Director

QFR Submitted by <u>Garamendi, John</u>
Subcommittee on Strategic Forces
JOINT (HASC-SF/HFAC-TNT) Hearing: Russian Arms Control
Cheating and the Administration's Responses
Wednesday, December 10, 2014

Questions for: <u>The Honorable Rose Gottemoeller</u>

1. Under Secretary Gottemoeller, you were asked a series of question about the various treaties and agreements by Representative Turner during the hearing, and you were compelled to answer yes or no, but you were not provided the opportunity to fully answer these questions. Congress should be fully informed about some very complex matters, and we need to get full answers to understand these complex issues. To the extent possible, could you please for the record provide the additional contextual information that this committee needs to fully understand the answers to your question regarding the status of Russia's compliance with the several treaties Representative Turner asked you about during the hearing, including the CWC, BWC, INF Treaty, CFE, New START, Treaty on Open Skies, the Vienna Document, Moratorium on Nuclear Testing, the Missile Technology Control Regime, and Budapest Memorandum? Is there any other additional information about these or other treaties that we should know about?

The response is classified and has been retained in committee files.

2. Page 52, Line 1232

The response is classified and has been retained in committee files.

QFR Submitted by <u>Turner, Michael R.</u>
Subcommittee on Strategic Forces
JOINT (HASC-SF/HFAC-TNT) Hearing: Russian Arms Control
Cheating and the Administration's Responses
Wednesday, December 10, 2014

Question for: <u>The Honorable Rose Gottemoeller</u>

1. Please describe why Russia is deploying first strike weapons like the Club-K system as well as the sea-launched land-attack cruise missile on the ultra-quiet Severodinsk nuclear submarine?
   a. How do these systems promote strategic stability?
   b. How is DOD preparing to counter these capabilities?

   While it is well known through various public statements by Russian leadership that Russia is undergoing broad military modernization, the Department of Defense will provide a separate, classified response to this question.
   The United States remains committed to maintain strategic stability between the United States and Russia and encouraging mutual steps to foster a more stable, resilient, predictable, and transparent security relationship, and to avoid the action-reaction cycle of an arms race.

Question for: <u>The Honorable Brian McKeon</u>

2. Please describe why Russia is deploying first strike weapons like the Club-K system as well as the sea-launched land-attack cruise missile on the ultra-quiet Severodinsk nuclear submarine?
   a. How do these systems promote strategic stability?
   b. How is DOD preparing to counter these capabilities?

   The response is classified and has been retained in committee files.

Question for: <u>The Honorable Rose Gottemoeller</u>

3. During the hearing, we discussed a series of treaties and agreements to which Russia is a party. Have you, upon further review, found any other treaties for agreements (e.g., the Open Skies Treaty, the Moratorium on Nuclear Testing, the Presidential Nuclear Initiatives, etc.) that you wish to clarify the status of Russia's compliance?
   a. Would you want to revise any of your answers from the hearing (for example, regarding the Vienna Document)?

b. Please provide us both a classified and unclassified list of all arms control treaties and agreements to which Russia is a party and the Administration's judgment regarding whether Russia is in compliance with each, in violation, or whether compliance cannot be verified. Please describe why certain findings are kept classified and why others are not.

c. Please provide an unclassified statement on the Administration's position regarding, in total, how many arms control treaties/agreements Russia is party to and how many of such treaties/agreements Russia is in compliance with.

The response is classified and has been retained in committee files.

QFR Submitted by <u>Rogers, Mike</u>
Subcommittee on Strategic Forces
JOINT (HASC-SF/HFAC-TNT) Hearing: Russian Arms Control
Cheating and the Administration's Responses
Wednesday, December 10, 2014

Question for: <u>The Honorable Rose Gottemoeller</u>

1. Has Russia deployed its new INF violating GLCM?
   a. Is there a difference between the "deployment" of such a missile and its having achieved initial operating capability?

The response is classified and has been retained in committee files.

Question for: <u>The Honorable Rose Gottemoeller</u>

2. According to Russian press accounts, Russian INF treaty non-compliance may have begun as early as 2008.
   a. When were you first concerned about possible Russian non-compliance with INF, and when did you or another senior State Department official first raise the issue of INF Treaty compliance with your Russian counterparts? NATO counterparts?

The response is classified and has been retained in committee files.

Question for: <u>The Honorable Rose Gottemoeller</u>

3. In international law and arms control practice, what is the significance of a "material breach"?
   a. What are some of the factors that constitute a "material breach"?
   b. What is the object and purpose of the INF treaty? Has that been defeated by Russian actions?
   c. What is the trigger for termination of INF? Since it is clear that it is not the testing of a missile that violates the treaty, is it deployment of a missile that violates the treaty? What about 10 illegal INF missiles are deployed? What about 20? 50? Is there a point where you would recommend the President terminate the treaty?

The international legal doctrine of material breach allows one party to suspend or terminate a treaty based on another party's "violation of a provision essential to the accomplishment of the object and purpose of the treaty." (Paragraph 3(b) of Article 60 of the Vienna Convention on the Law of Treaties). We of course have extremely serious concerns about

Russia's violation of the INF Treaty's ban on the possession, production, and flight-testing of intermediate range missiles. However, we do not believe it is in our interest to suspend the INF Treaty at this time. As a result, we have not invoked the doctrine of material breach. Our current efforts are focused on convincing Russia to return to compliance and preserving the viability of the INF Treaty, which we believe continues to serve U.S. and allied interests.

Question for: <u>The Honorable Brian McKeon</u>

4. In international law and arms control practice, what is the significance of a "material breach"?
    a. What are some of the factors that constitute a "material breach"?
    b. What is the object and purpose of the INF treaty? Has that been defeated by Russian actions?
    c. What is the trigger for termination of INF? Since it is clear that it is not the testing of a missile that violates the treaty, is it deployment of a missile that violates the treaty? What about 10 illegal INF missiles are deployed? What about 20? 50? Is there a point where you would recommend the President terminate the treaty?

The international legal doctrine of material breach allows one party to suspend or terminate a treaty based on another party's "violation of a provision essential to the accomplishment of the object and purpose of the treaty." (Paragraph 3(b) of Article 60 of the Vienna Convention on the Law of Treaties).

We of course have extremely serious concerns about Russia's violation of the INF Treaty's ban on the possession, production, and flight-testing of intermediate range missiles. However, we do not believe it is in our interest to suspend the INF Treaty at this time. As a result, we have not invoked the doctrine of material breach. Our current efforts are focused on convincing Russia to return to compliance and preserving the viability of the INF Treaty, which we believe continues to serve U.S. and allied interests. If Russia does not return to verifiable compliance, our goal will be to ensure that Russia gains no significant military advantage from its violation of INF Treaty obligations.

Question for: <u>The Honorable Rose Gottemoeller</u>

5. Is Russia deploying or preparing to deploy tactical nuclear weapons to Crimea? Is there a United States government view on whether Russia is planning to undertake such a deployment?
    a. Has the Administration shared such view with NATO?
    b. We clearly have direct statements by Russian leaders, including the chief kleptocrat, Mr. Putin, that Russia is preparing to put tactical nuclear weapons into

Crimea. Have we told NATO whether or not we agree that they are doing or preparing to do this?

We have seen unverified media reports about possible deployment in Crimea of dual capable delivery systems by the Russian armed forces. Any steps toward deploying nuclear weapons in Crimea would be destabilizing to European security and further transgress Ukraine's sovereignty and territorial integrity.

We consult regularly with NATO Allies on issues affecting our common security. The Administration will continue to work closely with allies and partners in Europe and internationally to respond to events in Ukraine and to support Ukraine's sovereignty and territorial integrity.

Question for: The Honorable Brian McKeon

6. Is Russia deploying or preparing to deploy tactical nuclear weapons to Crimea? Is there a United States government view on whether Russia is planning to undertake such a deployment?
   a. Has the Administration shared such view with NATO?
   b. We clearly have direct statements by Russian leaders, including the chief kleptocrat, Mr. Putin, that Russia is preparing to put tactical nuclear weapons into Crimea. Have we told NATO whether or not we agree that they are doing or preparing to do this?

We have also seen media reports that Russia is considering deployment of nuclear weapons in Crimea. To date, we have no indication that there are nuclear weapons in Crimea.

The United States has urged Russia not to deploy nuclear weapons to Crimea. Such a move would be a continued and escalatory violation of Ukraine's sovereignty and territorial integrity. Any steps toward deploying nuclear weapons in Crimea would further destabilize Europe and increase our concern, and that of our allies, about Russian actions in Eastern Europe.

The United States has kept its allies informed of this matter.

Question for: The Honorable Rose Gottemoeller

7. Has Russia tested its new RS-26 ballistic missile at intermediate ranges?
   a. I'm told the interagency decided to agree that this missile is an ICBM, notwithstanding a lengthy public record of intermediate-range flights with different warhead configurations, which was clearly contemplated as a scenario when in the INF treaty was ratified. I'm told we decided that we'd rather have these count under New START. How can we be confident Russia will allow itself

to be limited in that way? Is it because of their stellar record of compliance with arms control?

The response is classified and has been retained in committee files.

Question for: The Honorable Rose Gottemoeller

8. You remarked at a November missile defense conference in Romania that Russia has 68 missile defense interceptors and we will have 44. Are ours nuclear? Are theirs? Does that matter in terms of effect? Were you comparing apples to oranges?
    a. Did you take the opportunity of being in Romania to assure this key ally about U.S. efforts to respond to the INF treaty? With whom in the Romanian government did you meet to discuss Russia's violation?
    b. Has Russia sustained and modernized its BMD systems for national defense? If so, when, and why do you believe Russia has done this? And, why do Russian leaders continually label US BMD "destabilizing" while saying nothing about Russia's own systems?
    c. Do Russia's policies with regard to Russian missile defense appear to be driven by the goal of stability?

U.S. Ground-Based Interceptors (GBIs) deployed in Alaska and California, as well as the SM-3 interceptors that will be deployed to Romania and Poland, are not armed with a nuclear or conventional warhead but instead rely on "hit-to-kill" technology to destroy adversary ballistic missiles. The Russian strategic missile defense system—which is deployed around Moscow—includes the "Gazelle" interceptors which, according to open sources, can be armed with nuclear warheads. The detonation of a nuclear warhead in the atmosphere would have serious detrimental effects on the environment.

Russia has publically declared that they are sustaining and modernizing their missile defense systems. The Russian Government has also stated that these systems are designed to defend Moscow against nuclear strikes. We do not believe that Russia's Moscow ABM defenses or U.S. BMD are destabilizing.

We have and will continue to coordinate our response to Russia's violation of the INF Treaty with Romania and our other NATO Allies.

Question for: The Honorable Rose Gottemoeller

9. How many times have you discussed INF with your counterparts since the compliance report came out?
    a. How many times has Secretary Kerry? Has he ever directly raised the INF treaty with his counterpart?

    b. Has the President raised Russia's violation of the INF treaty with Russia's ruler?

The response is classified and has been retained in committee files.

Question for: The Honorable Rose Gottemoeller

10. Please describe economic sanctions we are considering concerning the INF treaty? Can you assure us our sanctions on Russian entities will have a direct economic consequence on Russia? Has that been calculated? What is the impact in dollars? How will these entities current business activities in the U.S. be affected?

In addition to our diplomatic efforts, the United States is actively reviewing and consulting with allies about potential economic measures in response to Russia's violation of the INF Treaty.

    While we cannot state an exact dollar impact of economic measures that have not been put in place, the possible measures will have direct economic consequence for the Russian Federation.

Question for: The Honorable Rose Gottemoeller

11. Please explain to me how the Administration can continue to talk about being interested in pursuing further nuclear arms reductions with Russia given the invasion of Ukraine (and continued violations of its sovereignty) and the violation of the INF treaty.
    a. During the consideration of the SALT II agreement, President Carter wrote to the Senate Majority Leader (available on page 10) and urged that the Senate not take up that treaty for ratification due to the Soviet invasion of Afghanistan. Is the Russian invasion of Ukraine less concerning than the Soviet invasion of Ukraine?
    b. How can you ask the Congress to trust Russia when it is not in compliance with at least eight of its arms control treaty obligations and agreements?

Russia's ongoing violations of Ukrainian sovereignty and territorial integrity, including its attempted annexation of Crimea and destabilizing activities in eastern Ukraine, are part of a pattern of action that is undermining stability and security in Europe and threatens the post-Cold war world order. Russia must implement in full the Minsk agreements to which it has signed up, including withdrawal of Russian troops and equipment and restoring Ukrainian sovereignty to the Ukraine-Russia border along with monitoring by the OSCE; a halt to separatist violations of the ceasefire and end to the violence; the end of Russian military support to the separatists; the release of all hostages including the pilot and parliament member Nadiya Savchenko and Ukrainian film producer Oleg Sentsov. Likewise, Russia must respect the parameters of the Budapest Memorandum and Minsk Agreements.

In light of Russia's attempted annexation of Crimea and destabilizing activities in eastern Ukraine, as well as Russia's lack of compliance with arms control treaties and agreements, including its violation of the INF Treaty, the Administration is reviewing its entire policy toward the Russian Federation. While the Administration is open to seeking negotiated reductions in nuclear weapons with the Russian Federation, such negotiations require a willing partner and a conducive environment, which are currently unavailable.

However, we need to remember that even in the darkest days of the Cold War, the United States and Soviet Union found it in our mutual interest to work together on reducing the nuclear threat. The system of arms control and nonproliferation treaties and agreements we maintain with the Russian Federation continue to be in the U.S. national security interest. The United States is committed to maintaining strategic stability between the United States and Russia and encourages mutual steps to foster a more stable, resilient, and transparent security relationship.

Question for: The Honorable Brian McKeon

12. Please explain to me how the Administration can continue to talk about being interested in pursuing further nuclear arms reductions with Russia given the invasion of Ukraine (and continued violations of its sovereignty) and the violation of the INF treaty.
   a. During the consideration of the SALT II agreement , President Carter wrote to the Senate Majority Leader (available on page 10) and urged that the Senate not take up that treaty for ratification due to the Soviet invasion of Afghanistan. Is the Russian invasion of Ukraine less concerning than the Soviet invasion of Ukraine?

   Russia's ongoing aggressive and destabilizing actions in eastern Ukraine as well as occupation and attempted annexation of Crimea is a serious matter. Russia's ongoing violations of Ukrainian sovereignty and territorial integrity are part of a pattern of action that is undermining stability and security in Europe and threatens the post-Cold War world order.

   b. How can you ask the Congress to trust Russia when it is not in compliance with at least eight of its arms control treaty obligations and agreements?

   In light of recent events in Ukraine, including Crimea, and Russia's lack of compliance with a number of arms control treaties and agreements, including its violation of the INF Treaty, the Administration is reviewing its entire policy toward the Russian Federation. To be sure, the current situation has significantly undermined mutual trust with the Russian Federation. We are not asking Congress to trust Russia. We are deeply concerned about Russian violations, and are pursuing an approach designed to bring Russia back into compliance with its obligations.

THE WHITE HOUSE
WASHINGTON

January 3, 1980

Dear Senator Byrd:

In light of the Soviet invasion of Afghanistan,
I request that you delay consideration of the
SALT II Treaty on the Senate floor.

The purpose of this request is not to withdraw
the Treaty from consideration, but to defer the
debate so that the Congress and I as President
can assess Soviet actions and intentions, and
devote our primary attention to the legislative
and other measures required to respond to this
crisis.

As you know, I continue to share your view
that the SALT II Treaty is in the national
security interest of the United States and the
entire world, and that it should be taken up
by the Senate as soon as these more urgent issues
have been addressed.

Sincerely,

Jimmy Carter

The Honorable Robert Byrd
Majority Leader of the United States Senate
Washington, D.C.

Question for: <u>The Honorable Brian McKeon</u>

13. The Chairman of the Joint Chiefs of Staff has stated there are military requirements on the books today (insert report for the record) that could be satisfied I the United States was not bound by the INF treaty. How long should the U.S. forego such required military capabilities if the Russian Federation is not going to be bound by the treaty?

The Chairman's Report on Conventional Prompt Global Strike Options if Exempt from the Restrictions of the Intermediate-Range Nuclear Forces (INF) Treaty listed four types of weapons systems that, in the absence of the INF Treaty, could assist in closing an existing Joint Requirements Oversight Council (JROC)-validated capability gap.

Although it is foreseeable that U.S. development and deployment of new military capabilities could enhance our strategic position vis-a-vis rival States by bolstering our deterrent and extended deterrent capabilities, the Department of Defense continues to believe that mutual compliance to the INF Treaty would provide more benefit and stability to the United States, its allies and partners, and the Russia Federation.

It is for this reason that the Administration is reviewing a broad range of diplomatic, economic, and military response options and considering the effect each of these options could have on convincing Russian leadership to return to compliance with the INF Treaty.

The Administration's goal is to convince Russia to return to verifiable compliance because we believe that preserving the INF Treaty is in our mutual security interest and that of our allies and partners. If Russia does not return to verifiable compliance, our goal will be to ensure that Russia gains no significant military advantage from its violation of INF Treaty obligations. The military responses we are currently considering would seek to negate any military advantage Russia might gain from deploying an INF Treaty-prohibited system.

Question for: <u>The Honorable Rose Gottemoeller</u>

14. What is the position of the Department of State concerning a "moratorium on testing of direct ascent kinetic energy ASAT weapons"?
    a. Have you authorized your personnel to negotiate such an agreement with foreign parties?

As I noted at the hearing, the Department of State and the Interagency looked at a moratorium as a potential diplomatic option to pursue to address anti-satellite (ASAT) programs of concern, but we are not placing emphasis on it at this time. Further, while we discuss a wide variety of space security issues with allies – including the potential for an International Code of Conduct and ways to address the development of ASAT systems – we have not made a specific proposal to allies for negotiation of a debris-generating ASAT testing moratorium. As a result, no C-175 package has been prepared.

Question for: <u>The Honorable Brian McKeon</u>

15. Has the Department of Defense considered the impacts of such a "moratoria"? What is the DOD position?

The Department of Defense has discussed that moratorium concept with the Department of State and other interagency partners and agrees with the decision not to pursue it at this time.

Question for: <u>The Honorable Rose Gottemoeller</u>

16. Does the Department of State agree with the 2010 Nuclear Posture Review that, "[t]he NPR considered the possibility of reducing alert rates for ICBMs and at-sea rates of SSBNs, and concluded that such steps could reduce crisis stability by giving an adversary the incentive to attack before 're-alerting' was complete"?
    a. Do you agree that alert rates should not be changed?

Yes. The Department of State participated fully in the development of the 2010 Nuclear Posture Review, and I support all of its conclusions.

Question for: <u>The Honorable Brian McKeon</u>

17. Does the Department of State agree with the 2010 Nuclear Posture Review that, "[t]he NPR considered the possibility of reducing alert rates for ICBMs and at-sea rates of SSBNs, and concluded that such steps could reduce crisis stability by giving an adversary the incentive to attack before 're-alerting' was complete"?
    a. Do you agree that alert rates should not be changed?

I cannot speak for the Department of State, but it is my understanding that the Department of State was a full participant in the Nuclear Posture Review, which was approved by the President. As then-Secretary Gates noted in his letter introducing the report of the review, "[f]rom beginning to end, this review was an interagency effort..."

From a DoD perspective, a U.S. decision to reduce alert rates would bring two distinct risks if a crisis were to emerge that required re-alerting. First, a decision by the President to re-alert would be visible to the adversary giving it an incentive to strike early, as mentioned in the NPR. Second, concern over escalatory re-alerting might drive the President to delay or forego re-alerting, thereby leaving the United States vulnerable not only to a large adversary strike, but to even a smaller attack intended to "decapitate" the ability of the United States to control its nuclear forces. The risk that the United States takes in both situations is too great to warrant taking this seemingly innocuous action, even during peacetime. As a result, DoD does not support changing alert rates at this time.

Question for: <u>The Honorable Rose Gottemoeller</u>

18. Russia is building a series of first strike weapons, including its new cruise missile submarine, the "Severodinsk" class with its long-range land attack cruise missile, not to mention its "Club-K" cruise missile system, which is designed to be hidden aboard container cargo ships.
    a. Why is Russia preparing a variety of first strike capabilities? How do these capabilities promote stability?
    b. Russia is offering for sale the "Club-K" system at arms sales around the world. What are the consequences for Russia to selling such systems? Do you have a consequence in mind?

It is well known through various public statements by Russian leadership that Russia is undergoing a broad military modernization program. The Department of Defense will provide a separate, classified response to this question.

The United States is committed to maintaining strategic stability between the United States and Russia and encourages mutual steps to foster a more stable, resilient, and transparent security relationship, and to avoid the action-reaction cycle of an arms race.

Question for: <u>The Honorable Brian McKeon</u>

19. How is DOD responding to the rise in Russian first strike capability development and planning?

The response is classified and has been retained in committee files.

QFR Submitted by <u>Cooper, Jim</u>
Subcommittee on Strategic Forces
JOINT (HASC-SF/HFAC-TNT) Hearing: Russian Arms Control
Cheating and the Administration's Responses
Wednesday, December 10, 2014

Questions for: <u>The Honorable Rose Gottemoeller</u>

1. Do you believe we should stop any potential nuclear weapons reductions and negotiations if Russia is in non-compliance on its arms control obligations? Why not?

Although the current situation has significantly undermined mutual trust, no one should forget that even in the darkest days of the Cold War, the United States and Russia found it in our mutual interest to work together on reducing the nuclear threat. The system of arms control and nonproliferation treaties and agreements we maintain with the Russian Federation continues to be in the U.S. national security interest. For example, both sides are implementing the New START Treaty in a business-like manner; experience is demonstrating that the New START Treaty's verification regime works, and continues to promote transparency and predictability in the U.S. and Russian nuclear relationship. The United States is committed to maintaining strategic stability between the United States and Russia and encourages mutual steps to foster a more stable, resilient, and transparent security relationship. We remain committed to arms-control and will continue to urge Russia to return to verifiable compliance with its obligations.

Question for: <u>The Honorable Brian McKeon</u>

2. Do you believe we should stop any potential nuclear weapons reductions and negotiations if Russia is in non-compliance on its arms control obligations? Why not?

In light of recent events in Ukraine, including Crimea, and Russia's lack of compliance with a number of arms control treaties and agreements, including its violation of the INF Treaty, the Administration is reviewing its entire policy toward the Russian Federation. To be sure, the current situation has significantly undermined mutual trust with the Russian Federation. We are deeply concerned about Russian violations, and are pursuing an approach designed to bring Russia back into compliance with its obligations.

The Department of Defense continues to believe that mutual compliance with nuclear arms control agreements can provide benefit and stability to the United States, its allies and partners, and the Russia Federation.

Questions for: <u>The Honorable Rose Gottemoeller</u>

3. What do you recommend the U.S. does in response to such cheating? What is the appropriate role for the Congress in response to such cheating? What are our options for bringing Russia back into compliance with the treaty? How effective is each option? Which is most effective?

We must continue to engage Russia diplomatically in addressing its violation of its INF Treaty obligations and returning Russia to compliance with its Treaty obligations. We are considering a range of appropriate options – diplomatic, economic, and military – to respond to Russia's continuing violation of its treaty obligations. The United States should speak with a single voice to demonstrate resolve as we continue to engage Russia diplomatically and explore measures to bring Russia back into compliance. Additionally, we've briefed our allies on our concerns and will continue to coordinate with them on this and other matters that affect our common security.

Question for: <u>The Honorable Brian McKeon</u>

4. What do you recommend the U.S. does in response to such cheating? What is the appropriate role for the Congress in response to such cheating? What are our options for bringing Russia back into compliance with the treaty? How effective is each option? Which is most effective?

The Administration is reviewing a broad range of diplomatic, economic, and military response options and considering the effect each of these options could have on convincing Russian leadership to return to compliance with the INF Treaty.

Although it is foreseeable that U.S. development and deployment of new military capabilities could enhance our strategic position vis-a-vis rival States by bolstering our deterrent and extended deterrent capabilities, the Department of Defense continues to believe that mutual compliance to the INF Treaty would provide more benefit and stability to the United States, its allies and partners, and the Russia Federation.

The Administration's goal is to convince Russia to return to verifiable compliance because we believe that preserving the INF Treaty is in our mutual security interest and that of our allies and partners. If Russia does not return to verifiable compliance, our goal will be to ensure that Russia gains no significant military advantage from its violation of INF Treaty obligations, and the military options that we are currently considering would seek to do that.